Switched At Birth

Frederick J. George

Published by Frederick J. George

Second Edition

To both my families

In loving memory of
Ngaire Agnes Edwards George,
the loving mother who raised me;
of John George,
The father who gave me his name
And his heritage;
Of Michael and Paul George,
The brothers I grew up with;
Of Gordon Churchman,
The father I never knew;
Of Maxwell Churchman,
The brother I never met.

And for Helen Grace Somerville Churchman,
The true mother God has given me
To know and to love.

Contents

Chapter 1   *A Huge Secret Revealed*   Page 1

Chapter 2   *The Georges*   Page 9

Chapter 3   *The Churchman's and the   Page 22
             Somerville's*

Chapter 4   *A Little Background*   Page 32

Chapter 5   *Boys Will Be Boys…. Apparently*   Page 39

Chapter 6   *The First Doubts*   Page 64

Chapter 7   *Hobbies, Occupations, The Army and   Page 80
             Altercations*

Chapter 8   *Rugby, and How It Led to My   Page 118
             Marriage*

Chapter 9   *A Family of My Own*   Page 132

Chapter 10   *Confirming the Switch…   Page 185
             And Then What?*

Chapter One

A Huge Secret Revealed

Once upon a time down on the farm where a duck family lived, Mother Duck had been sitting on a clutch of new eggs. One nice morning, the eggs hatched and out popped six chirpy ducklings. But one egg was bigger than the rest, and it didn't hatch. Mother Duck couldn't recall laying that seventh egg.

From the day the final egg hatched, the little bird that came out was different than Mother Duck and the ducklings. He became known as the Ugly Duckling and grew up wondering why he was so different, why he didn't fit in … what was wrong with him? In the happy ending of this fairy tale written by Hans Christian Anderson we learn that nothing was wrong after all. The Ugly Duckling was not a duckling, after all, but a swan.

Growing up I was the Ugly Duckling in my family. All my brothers and sisters had dark features and displayed rambunctious, confident personalities while I had lighter hair and was quiet and shy. I was so different that my father – sometimes in jest, sometimes not – often suggested that the Ugly Duckling in our family was the product of my mother having an affair. My father never knew what to do with me but mom took this duckling under her wing and loved me.

As a young boy growing up in a Lebanese family I always had strange feelings about whom I was and wondered why I was different than the others. While my brothers laughed and joked and did silly things, I was more reserved and withdrawn. It was puzzling. This feeling of not belonging was aggravated when my older brother's best friend, Jim, started hanging around our house and neighborhood. Jim fit in so easily with my parents, brothers and sisters that he seemed like one of the family. Why, than, was it so hard for me to fit in?

When I was two-years-old I was inflicted by a medical condition that doctors said could keep me from walking. I had my leg in plaster until I was five-years-old. Mom got me through this hurdle and set the example I would follow throughout my life – when life hands you a hurdle, jump it! With mom's help, I kept walking and then sprinted and then ran so that later in life I would run the Boston Marathon in just a little over three hours. Mom's persistent encouragement reminds me of the song Bette Middler sang, "Wind Beneath My Wings," as she inspired me and still does today, even though Ngaire George, died in 1970.

Because my life has been seemingly ruled by fate I have learned to play the cards I've been dealt and get on with life so that fate influences, rather than controls, my life. The first time I met fate was just a few weeks after drawing my first breath but there's been several encounters since. More than once while driving my car fate got behind the wheel and steered me into a near-fatal accident. There were other "accidents" in my life also but I survived them all. This pattern has occurred often enough to convince me I am a survivor for a reason. I survived because there was this huge secret that would be kept from me for more than 50 years that had not yet been discovered!

There have been several remarkable "coincidences" in my life, like the impact the assassination of President Kennedy had on me as a New Zealand schoolboy and the fact that later in life I baked a wedding cake for the Kennedy family. Another is the fact that my father-in-law's commanding officer, Colonel Charlie Sweeney, flew the plane that dropped the atomic bomb over Japan and a developer of the atomic bomb, Hugh William Frederick Wilkins who also was born in New Zealand, is credited with developing the DNA process. And it was DNA years later that revealed the huge secret in my life.

The DNA test I took at age 56 revealed a huge secret that nothing was really wrong with me after all because I was a Churchman, not a George. I had been switched at birth and the family I came to love and cherish was not the family I belonged to. Ngaire George, the greatest person in the world to me, was not my birth mother after all. I had a family I had never met and the brothers and sisters I grew up with were not my blood family. After half a century of being a duckling, I learned I was a swan – I was not a George but a Churchman!

This is the Queen Mary Maternity Hospital where the mix-up between Jim and me took place. It is now a hostel for university students.

The "switch" occurred during the Christmas holiday season of 1946 when there were two babies born within two hours of each other. After both were removed for a diaper change and bath, the two babies were placed in baby carts in the hospital nursery. At this time there were no identification bracelets on babies' ankles or on mothers' wrists. And so the baby born to John and Ngaire at 11:55 p.m. December 23 was placed in the bassinet that was supposed to be occupied by James Francis Churchman. And the baby born to Gordon and Helen Churchman at 1:38 a.m. December 24 was placed in the bassinet intended for Frederick John George.

At one point my birth mother, Helen Churchman, said to the midwife: "I think you have given me the wrong baby." The midwife in charge and conducting nurse, whose name was J Pearson, just laughed and said don't be silly. Mrs. George's descendants included a Pearson family from Sweden (more about this later) but it's quite a coincidence that the midwife had the same name as Mrs. George's grandfather. My birth mother thought maybe the baby was a throwback to her Welsh relatives on her mother's side who tended to be darker in skin tone. Gordon Churchman the next day questioned the hospital staff and doctor about whether a switch had occurred and they all denied it. Ngaire George also wondered about my appearance and thought maybe I was a throwback to her Scandinavian side. To add to the confusion, my birth father Gordon Churchman's middle name was Pearson.

And so life went on for Jim Churchman and Fred George with one notable change – Jim became Fred and Fred became Jim. And that's how I became the fifth of 13 children in a Roman Catholic Lebanese family instead of the second of five in a Scottish Presbyterian family.

And so the mystery of the Ugly Duckling, as solved by Hans Christian Anderson, is now unraveling in my life as I learn to be a swan. The biggest change is an understanding of the power of genetics which controls much more than gender, hair and eye colors, height and weight. Our genes also impact our traits, habits, idiosyncrasies, skills, inclinations, and personality. I was a Churchman trying to act like a George, and the clash created by a swan living with ducklings produced a reaction as powerful and predictable as thunder and lightening bursting forth when two different weather fronts meet.

I've certainly had an unusual life as Frederick John George. I am 61-years-old now and the notion that I am not a George, but a Churchman, is still new to me. It won't change what my life has been and certainly won't change who or what I am. And yet it already has changed what my life is becoming. I have a whole new family, entirely new relationships, and new possibilities. And, of course, I have a new mother.

Helen Churchman is 87-years-old now. As it happens, she is the only one of the four parents who is still alive. We keep in pretty close touch as she writes to me every week. We are trying to get to know each other – this 87-year-old mother and her newly-discovered 61-year-old son! She is one of the reasons for this book. I want her to know her son; to know not just *that* I am, but to know *who* I am – the sum of my ancestry, my upbringing, all my relations, all my experiences. I don't expect to displace Jim because I know that there is room enough in her heart for us both.

Three months after the George/Churchman baby switch, there almost was another baby switch in the same New Zealand hospital where I was born. This was a case of a woman whose newborn baby girl had nearly been switched. The mother being handed a baby boy protested because she actually had given birth to a girl. Without that instantaneous protest another switch would have occurred. Because of that "near-switch" the hospital created a new policy and began putting identification bracelets on the ankles of all newborn babies.

There have been other stories in addition to mine of babies switched at birth. In May 2008 CBS told the story on 48 Hours of a baby, Shirley Morgan, who was switched in the hospital shortly after birth. The father, Jim Morgan, always suspected something was wrong but the mother and other family members decided Shirley's darker facial color was due to a great-grandmother who was French Canadian and had similar coloring. At age 80, Jim suffered a serious heart attack and was taken to a nursing home. On his death bed, Jim Morgan again shared his fear that Shirley was not his child. Another daughter (Kathy) arranged DNA tests for her father, mother and Shirley. The DNA tests revealed, 43 years after the fact, that Shirley had been switched at birth!

On the Canary Island a lawsuit was filed in 2004 for damages resulting from identical twin sisters being separated from each other in the hospital in 1973. The one twin was taken out of her hospital crib and then was mistakenly replaced by another baby girl whom the family raised. In 2001 the twin separated from her sister at birth walked into a clothing store on the island where the switch had occurred. A sales assistant was friends with the other twin whom she usually greeted with a kiss. So on this day she greeted the other twin with a kiss and was completely ignored. So she called her friend (the other twin) who told her she had not been in the store that day. The store clerk arranged a meeting to have the three girls take DNA tests confirmed the women were identical twins and, of course, the DNA of the third girl who had been placed in the wrong cot did not match with the twins.

Shirley Morgan is struggling with the challenge of adjusting to a new family. Kathy Morgan is ready to move on with her life and to work hard on becoming acquainted with her new sister. The identical twin raised by the wrong family wishes she had never learned the truth. These two stories, and mine, reveal that the fallout from being switched at birth has traumatic effects that ripple through entire families, effecting different people in different ways. Before taking a look at the fallout in my families, let me first tell you about the Georges and the Churchman/Somerville families.

Chapter Two

The Georges

The Georges are a Lebanese family who grew up in part of the larger Lebanese community within the city of Dunedin, on New Zealand's South Island. Stories of the old homeland, and the Lebanese customs and traditions were passed down, and maintained for many years. Their heritage provided a stability and sense of pride for many of the immigrant families.

My mother, Ngaire Agnes Edwards George, actually was not Lebanese. She grew up in Dannevirke near Hastings on the North Island of New Zealand. In February 1931 she survived the worst earthquake New Zealand ever had. The center of the quake, north of Napier, measured 7.9 on the Richter scale. Some 256 people were killed. My mother narrowly escaped. Because it was so cold that night she slept in her family's bungalow instead of inside the brick bungalow which came crashing down on her bed where she would have been sleeping.

Ngaire Edwards was a lively, attractive young woman. She had many friends – one of whom was Jessie George, John George's youngest sister. That's how my parents met. They were married in Ngaire's home – in a Roman Catholic service -- even though the Edwards were Protestant.

So she married into the George family, and it was as if she had always been a George – except for the religion issue. She was a pretty independent person who did not want to have her life dictated by the influence of the Lebanese culture and Roman Catholic religion. She wanted our love for herself -- for what she was -- and we each gave her our love in our own way. She was always supportive of us and the things we did, whether it was playing sports or finding a job. I couldn't have wished for a better mother.

The Georges originally came from a small mountain village in Lebanon -- Bsharry. The name is biblical, meaning "milky white," and it refers to the snow-covered cedars of the Lebanon Mountains. Villagers tended sheep, and also vines, figs, cherries, olives, and mulberries. The little village -- almost hidden in the mountains -- had provided a place of refuge for Christians for many generations. Over the years the population began to grow but the opportunities for a good livelihood did not. So, beginning in the late 1800s, some of the population of Bscharry boarded ships to sail to new lives in other countries. Many went to the Americas, a few to Australia, and a handful even further to New Zealand and other places in the world. Bsharry is the birth place of the famous poet and prophet Kahlil Gibran whom lived in Boston became quite famous for his poems and drawings.

The Lebanese settled in clusters in Dunedin, a city on the lower southeast side of the South Island. When they first moved to Dunedin, they tended to stay together. And they settled in what was regarded as a pretty disreputable part of the city -- Walker Street which is now Carroll Street. At that time there was a lot of illegal gambling and prostitution on Walker Street. The Lebanese also had to deal with some pretty tough ethnic bigotry. But as a whole, the Lebanese were quite religious, family-oriented people who hung onto the extremely high principles they brought with them from the old country, and they made out all right.

Today Dunedin is the fourth-largest city in New Zealand, and the Lebanese community continues to flourish there. They have an annual picnic and a social club in the middle of the city, called the Cedar Club. In 1862 there was a gold rush in central Otago, so at one point this was a prosperous area.

Taken when Dunedin was first settled - which would be the late 1800's.
Shows you how tough it was.

Larnarch Castle.
This castle belonged to a member of Parliament. It is up on the hill off Portabello Road,
coming into one of the most spectacular entrances to any harbor in the world.
Mr. Larnach had tile ceilings put in the rooms of this castle which was unheard of, he
had a few wives, he committed suicide and is buried in the Dunedin central cemetery.

My grandparents were Nora and Joseph George. (*I grew up regarding all the Georges as my family so I won't change those references. When I talk about the Churchman family, I will specify them as such*). My grandparents settled on a farm 38 miles south of Dunedin, in an area known as the Catlins, a spectacular beautiful scenic area on the south coast of Otago. When a ship ran aground off shore, my grandfather helped bring the people to safety, providing them with blankets and creating a fire to keep them warm until help arrived. The Tory Government did not even thank him. Due to economics he lost his farm. They had died by the time I was two so I do not remember them.

The "George" surname comes from a Lebanese tradition whereby the son would take the first name of his father when he left home to go to another country. As in my grandfather's case his surname came from his father whose full name was Geryes Boulos Fakhry. George is English for Geryes so his name became Joseph George when he arrived in New Zealand.

This is one of the George/Churchman/Somerville coincidences. Only a few years before the Georges settled in the Catlins, and only a few miles away from what became my great-great uncle's farm, John and James Somerville (who was my birth mother Helen Somerville Churchman's great uncle) established the first flour mill in Otago. The mill turned into a pretty large operation, with a butcher shop attached. At one point, there were 40 people working at the mill. But they ran into cash flow problems because the local trade was based on the barter system, and went out of business.

Anyhow, Joseph and Nora George settled in the Otago province with their six children. My father was the fourth child, and the first son. We knew his sisters as Aunty Kate, Aunty Jean, and Aunty Margaret. Then there was Uncle Joe and Aunty Jessie.

As the oldest boy, my father would have inherited the farm. But farming was too tough a life for my father who especially didn't relish getting up early every morning to milk cows. So he decided to move to the city.

My grandparents - Nora and Joseph George

Dad had no trouble settling into the Lebanese community in Dunedin. And eventually my father's two older sisters moved to Dunedin, too. Aunty Kate went to live in Temuka, which is north of Dunedin. And Uncle Joe lived on Stafford Street in Dunedin, with his wife Julie. His parents (our grandparents) used to live in Dunedin. So the whole family stayed together.

Aunty Jean never married. Aunty Margaret married a man named Nick Barbara, and they had a son – my cousin George who was about a year younger than I. Nick died as a young man and Aunty Margaret was left to raise George by herself.

It's funny what you remember. I have this vivid memory of Aunty Margaret giving Georgie a bath. She had a big old portable tub which she used to put it in the middle of the kitchen table and fill with hot water from the coal range. Then she would bring Georgie in and give him a bath, right there while everybody's in the kitchen. He was little and didn't seem to mind but that scene still sticks in my mind.

Aunty Jean and Aunty Margaret later both worked at the hat factory on Stafford Street, just down the road from where they lived. Our school was close to the hat factory, so my brother Paul and I used to wait for our lunch break, and then go to see our aunts.

We did this often enough that, when we knocked on the workshop door, the woman who answered would just look at us and then call to Aunty Jean, *"Bring your purse Jean your nephews are here!"* We would ask her for money to buy fish and chips for lunch. (Back then in

New Zealand, fish and chips were just like American fast food -- not exactly healthy, but really good-tasting.)

Aunty Jean would always pull her purse out and give us the money we needed. Then she would say, "This is all I've got left. You took my last pennies! And the horse I bet on Saturday is still running!" And we would all laugh. No matter how many times we did it, she always said, "You took my last pennies," and we always laughed.

Both my aunts argued like crazy with each other, just like little kids. They would have these big fights, with a lot of hollering and yelling. Aunty Jean would have hot and cold flashes and sit there constantly fanning herself. And Aunty Margaret would yell at her, "You're driving me to the drink!" But it didn't really mean anything.

I remember one afternoon I went to visit them just after I had come back from the States. I still had my travel bag hung over my shoulder. Aunty Jean looked out the window and saw me coming. She hollered out to Aunty Margaret, "The mailman is here." And Aunty Margaret hollered back, "Don't be silly – the mailman doesn't come in the afternoon." They were starting to get in quite a "yes, it is; no, it isn't" argument when I walked inside the flat. When they recognized me, and realized what had happened, we all had a big laugh.

They always stuck together. And they preserved some of the old Lebanese ways. They kept house, for instance, in the old way, as clean-freaks. Everything was always neat and clean. When I walked in the house and sat down, one or the other would come up to me and say, "Lift your feet up." And she would go around with a little broom and dustpan and sweep the floor underneath where I was sitting. It was just like Blondie and Dagwood!

My aunts cooked the traditional Lebanese foods. I still remember the names of some of the dishes. *Salata* was the Lebanese word for salad (shredded lettuce put in a bowl with onions, tomatoes, red or green peppers, mint etc. mixed with olive oil, lemon juice and or vinegar, as olive oil was expensive mum would improvise and use melted butter). This applied to most recipes as the new immigrants would improvise to get by. The *salata* was mixed by hand, and served with mashed potatoes and sausages. What a meal! *Hahleeb* was milk, *soukkar* was sugar, *ma* was water, and *say* was tea. We really never learned to speak Lebanese, but we learned isolated words like *Sitti* for grandmother and Jiddi for grandfather. We learned some of the old Lebanese cuss-words, too, but nobody would translate them for us.

My aunts used olive oil, garlic, and crushed wheat a lot in their cooking. We used to buy the whole grain and they would crush it themselves. I don't remember actually seeing kids using sticks to scare the birds away from the sacks of wheat that were drying in the backyard, but I heard about it.

Aunty Jean and Aunty Margaret would make a kind of casserole, *kibbeh*, from mutton, crushed wheat, and seasonings. And they made *tabbouleh*, from crushed wheat with garlic, lemon juice, parsley and mint.

Aunty Jean's favorite, though, was *ma'shi*. I can taste it to this day. It was a kind of stuffed cabbage. Aunty Jean would mix mince and rice together, season it up with garlic, and put spoonfuls of the mix in cabbage leaves. Then she folded the leaves, covered them with lemon juice, and let them soak overnight. It sure was good, and we always looked forward to the times when Aunty Jean made *ma'shie*.

Aunty Margaret and Aunty Jean

Aunty Jean and Aunty Margaret died a long time ago. They both had kind hearts. I miss them a lot.

My father worked a lot of different laborer jobs once he got to Dunedin. He drove trucks and did freezer work in the meat packing plant, the Burnside Freezing Works. He wasn't trained as a professional barber but did cut hair in a barber shop in Dunedin. It was a family joke that if Dad was going to cut your hair, you ran for your life because dad used sheep shearing razors. Some days you got away but often he overtook you, grabbed you and dragged you back for your "haircut." When we told our friend Brian Bridges this he ran for his life for fear he too would get his hair cut.

Dad was a no-nonsense, rough-and-tumble man who loved having fun, playing cards, betting on horse races and dancing. He did not drink too much. He called booze "giggly juice," and didn't trust it. Dad used to say to us *"What good is it if a man gains the whole world but loses his soul"*. Another saying was *"Make hay while the sun shines."*

Dad and Mum saw that we practiced our religion. We used to say the rosary every night – on our knees with Aunty Jean. And my sister Myra would take me to mass. I remember that I fainted one morning, partway through the mass. This, of course, was back in the days when you were not allowed to eat before you received the holy sacraments. (There were other rules, too, -- some written down and some just understood. You couldn't eat meat on Friday, women had to wear hats in church, and they always wore skirts or dresses. How times have changed!)

My dad was like the other Lebanese – quite emotional, volatile, sometimes reckless, but with incredibly strong feelings for family and heritage.

Everything was Lebanese when I was growing up. That had both good and not-so-good aspects to it. For instance, Dad wanted all of us boys to marry Lebanese girls but not one of us did! Along with being emotionally unpredictable, the Lebanese are typically extremely warm people – they take you to their hearts, and are not shy or inhibited. And, most of all, they're always a lot of fun.

Milham (Malcolm) Michael came from Lebanon and married my dad's sister, Mary. They had 11 children. I had a lot of respect for him because he would always ask us how our mother was. Uncle Malcolm was quite a religious man. You would often see him carrying a sack of potatoes up a steep street in Dunedin as he said his prayers with rosary beads in his hand. His son, David, would be walking behind him reading the race book.

Another story about Uncle Malcolm was about his daughter getting married. The priest officiating at the wedding was called Father Fakhry. There must have been at least 300 people at the reception and when my uncle started thanking everyone with his broken English he mentioned the priest's name with every second word and it sounded like he was swearing. Everyone was in stitches – except my uncle of course!

John and Ngaire George with 3-month old Francis in 1943

Katie (George) Langston – dad's sister

The George family in the late 1970s

Chapter Three

The Churchman's and the Somerville's

The Churchman's are an old New Zealand family, and the Somerville's (Helen Churchman's family) are older still. It's ironic that I know the more recent history of the George family but not much about any of their ancestors before my dad's parents. But it's different with the Churchman's and the Somerville's. I don't know much about the Churchman's at all. With the Somerville's I know about some of the early ancestors, and a little as far forward as Helen Churchman's grandparents, but I don't know much at all about the more recent family history.

The Somerville's originally came from France. The name "Somervill" comes from an area of Picardy called Somme Valley. Sir Gaulter de Somervill was one of the

Norman knights who went with William the Conqueror to England and took part in the Battle of Hastings in 1066. Sir Gaulter received the English baronies of Whichenour in Somerset and Ashton in Gloucestershire in reward for his service and loyalty. He became the first in a long line of Somervill barons. (William the Conqueror is the current Prince Charles's 27th great-grandfather.)

William de Somervill, a descendant of Sir Gaulter, settled in Scotland and received land in Lanarkshire from the Scottish king, David the First, around the year 1136. And it was this William de Somervill's son, John, who is said to have killed a monstrous worm, or serpent, which had ravaged the area around Linton. The legend has been told by many poets, historians, and novelists -- including Sir Walter Scott – but the best account may be from "The Memoir of the Somervills" written in 1825 by James, the 11th Lord Somervill.

The farmers in the district of Linton in Roxburghshire were greatly annoyed and alarmed by the appearance of a monster in the shape of a worm, or serpent. "In length," says Sir James, "three Scots yards (almost nine and a half feet), and bigger than an ordinary man's leg, with a head more proportional to its length than its size around." It was said that its very breath would make farm animals lie down and die.

Many attempts and schemes were tried to kill it, but all failed until John Somervill, one of the members of the court of King William the Lion, succeeded.

John Somervill designed a special weapon for dealing with the serpent. It was a long, extra-strong, iron-bound spear, at the end of which was attached a small wheel. Covering the wheel was burning peat, which had been saturated with pitch to prolong the burning.

The Scottish nobleman practiced for many days, accustoming his pony to the fire and perfecting the steadiness of his aim while riding full-tilt at a target. Finally satisfied with his skill, he rode to the serpent's den and began to make loud noises which roused the beast. Somervill waited until the serpent's head was well raised and its mouth open to seize him. He then spurred his pony into a full gallop, ran the spear with the burning peat down the throat of the monster, and left it there to die and rot.

John Somervill became a hero, and was made First Baron of Linton by the King in 1174. The site of the serpent's den is still known as Worm's Glen, and the field in which it is situated is called Wormington. There is a church in the Linton parish that bears the Somerville Stone, an ancient carving of a man on horseback, thrusting a long spear into the mouth of an animal resembling a dragon.

The inscription on the stone is no longer legible, but it once read:

The wode (angry) Laird of Larristone
Slew the Worme of Wormiston
And won all Linton parishes.

The most notable event to occur in the time of William, the second baron of Linton, was the tremendous increase in property owned by the family, which formed the foundation of the great territorial power the family long enjoyed in this part of Clydesdale. William's son, Walter, fought alongside Sir William Wallace and Sir Walter commanded the Third Brigade of Horse in the Battle of Biggar and won(a battle featured in Mel Gibson's blockbuster movie "Braveheart. " Sir Wallace died of wounds received in the battle and was not beheaded as depicted in the movie "Braveheart.")

Walter's son, John, following in his father's footsteps, fought under the banner of Robert the Bruce and was present at the victorious Battle of Bannockburn. As a result of service to their monarchs, and good management, further estates and baronies were accumulated until the zenith of the family fortunes was reached in the time of Thomas, who became baron in 1406.

The Somerville's were a large family with a lot of branches. There were Somerville's in England, Ireland, France, Canada, and America. Sometime in the 17th century around the Reformation, there were bitter religious quarrels within the family. And the upshot was the Catholic branch of the family spelled their name "Summerville "and the Protestant branch spelled their name "Somerville."

In the early 1800s New Zealand began to be settled by Europeans. There were Somervilles on the *Blundell*, one of the first ships to bring settlers over from Europe. John and Janet Somerville, who were first cousins, had ten children. One of the ten children was Helen Churchman's great-uncle Robert Somerville who printed the "Blundell Chronicle" fortnightly on the ship as it came from England to New Zealand.

William and Marion (Davidson) Somerville were Helen Churchman's grandparents. Helen's great-uncle John (second oldest of John and Janet) and Margaret Brown were married by the Reverend Thomas Burns, the spiritual leader of the Scottish settlers and a nephew of Scottish poet Robert Burns. And you'd never guess where Thomas Burns' church was located. The church was at the corner Frederick Street and George Street. My sister Lloma and her husband Graeme Penny were married in the Thomas Burns Church and I used to live diagonally across the road from the church in a flat above a bar called "Robbie Burns." Further, there is a statue of Robert Burns in the middle of Dunedin and another one in the middle of Quincy, Massachusetts − my first home when I moved to the United States. How weird is all that?

On their honeymoon, John and Margaret Somerville walked over quite a bit of uncleared land and somewhere in the 40-mile stretch between Dunedin and Milton, Margaret told her new husband that her feet were getting extremely sore. He suggested putting soap on them, to kind of grease them up. That seemed to work, but then after walking another few miles, he noticed that soap suds were bubbling out of her boots. The tale of the bubbling boots is an old Somerville family story that gets re-told every time the family gets together.

The place where John and Margaret settled was called either "Big Waverly" or "Little Waverly." Here's why. As they crossed streams, they would have to cut trees down and make a fragile roadway over the water. Because the roadway was not firm, it "wavered" back and forth when walked on. Waverly today is one of the suburbs of Dunedin.

I don't know much more about the family than this. Helen Churchman has told me that she and her future husband Gordon first became friends when they met at church – the Anderson's Bay Presbyterian Church – where both were attending a Bible class. She remembered noticing him because his mother kept him all bundled up in sweaters and other warm clothes, thinking he might catch cold. Otago had separate schools for boys and girls, but Helen remembers that Gordon was more persistent and ingenious in finding ways to be around her than were the other boys.

An amazing coincidence with the Churchman's and Somerville's is that my cousin Ken Dreaver is also a direct descendant of a Norman Knight, Lawrence De

Grant. My father Gordon Churchman married my mother, a Somerville, and his sister Dora married a Dreaver who was a direct descendant of Lawrence De Grant. Ulysses Simpson Grant, the 18th President of United States, is also a direct descendant of Lawrence De Grant

At concert in Plymouth, Mass., I met entertainer David Somerville. In the late 1950s David formed The Four Diamonds who became quite popular with hit songs like *Why Do Fools Fall in Love?* and *Li'l Darling*. The Four Diamonds toured with such big names as Buddy Holly, Chubby Checker, Everly Brothers, and Elvis Presley. I obtained David's autograph when we met. I don't know exactly what the family lines and connections are, but I'm sure they exist.

So maybe I'll eventually know as much about the Somervilles and the Churchmans as I know about the George family.

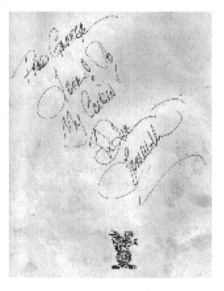

David Somerville's autograph.

The Somerville family.
Second from right – my birth mother – Helen as a young girl.

Gordon Churchman and Helen Somerville
married July 5, 1943

This is the Churchman Family - Jock, Jim (my switch),
Owen and Jane - minus Max and me of course.

Does that photo speak for itself?

This is the original house that the early Somervilles settled in near Somerville St. It is still there today. It just so happened that I lived near here as a George.

Uncle Jack – my birth mother's brother.

He was a Chaplin in WW11 he attended to the N.Z. soldiers' needs, who were fighting the Germans in Italy. He also was the Moderator for the Presbyterian Church in N.Z. The irony of this is I would not have set foot in any Protestant church growing up - shows you how much the switch at birth changed my life.

Chapter Four

A Little Background

There were 13 children in the George family. First came Myra, Francis, Nora, Michael, and me. Then came Paul and then the twins, Peter and Phillip, followed by Stephan, Lloma, Paulette, Neville and, last of all, Soraya.

There was a saying in our family that "the first one up was the best dressed and fed."

My mother was a real hero. She had health problems of her own but never failed to take care of her children. With 13 children there are bound to be two or three in some kind of behavioral or medical trouble at any given time. And I had more than my fair share of medical trouble.

Although my birth was normal and without complications by the time I was five weeks old I was having convulsions from a severe sinus infection. Two weeks later I developed hydrocephalus (water on the brain), and had to be "taken away." I don't know where I was taken away to as my mother didn't tell me about this until I was nearly 13-years-old. Apparently my hydrocephalus was pretty severe because one nurse said my head had swelled to 22 inches in diameter (it's now 19 inches!). The doctor, who turned out to have been a quack, said: "If this baby lives, he's going to be a vegetable." My mother didn't accept that, and had another doctor look at me. The second doctor said he knew what the problem was. According to my mother, the second doctor took me away and fixed the condition. I don't know anything more about it than this. I noticed later in life that I would need the largest size cap – guess I still have a swelled head!

The doctor who provided the misdiagnosis practiced in Dunedin for years. I would often walk past his office on my way my school, the Christian Brothers High School, (CBHS). Sometimes I would see the quack doctor who was then old and decrepit. I never said a word to him – it would have been a waste of time – but to think he could have sealed my fate boggles my mind.

There was a society called the Karitane nurses started by a doctor in the small resort town of Karitane outside of Dunedin. The nurses would visit the home of a woman who had had a baby. They would monitor the baby's progress and offer the new mother advice. They would pay regular visits until the baby was six months old. All this service was provided at no cost to the parents. I am sure it must have helped me.

There were a lot more illnesses, too. As a baby I had bronchitis and bronchial pneumonia. Then, when I was not quite two-years-old, I had tonsillitis, and my tonsils were taken out.

About the same time, the doctor noticed a deformity in my ankles, and my legs were put in plaster for 18 months. I didn't walk until I was four-years-old. The ankle deformity did not cause a lasting handicap, however, as years later I ran the Boston Marathon in a little more than three hours! I also ran in three other marathons, but I digress.

When I was two years old, I had to be admitted to the hospital for laryngitis. Then, two months later, I fell out of a moving car and just missed being run over by the city tram car. Four months after that, I was hospitalized for an upper respiratory infection. At the same time Jim Churchman was in the same hospital. He had spilled a pan of boiling fat onto himself.

After that, I was in and out of the hospital nearly every year. My tonsils grew back and had to be taken out again. I had repeated headaches and visits to the X-ray department. And, at about 12 years of age I had my appendix taken out. With a lovely red headed nurse taking my stitches out, so I did not mind.

Above: This tram car used to travel up and down High Street years ago. I was two years old when I fell out of the car and landed right where this taxi is (see below). The tram missed me by inches.

I didn't start talking until I was five-years-old, maybe because I had been so sick so often. My younger brother, Paul, taught me how to talk. When I did finally start to talk, I had a speech impediment. My mother took me to speech therapy classes in Caversham School, and I remember the teacher telling me to keep my tongue between my teeth when I spoke the *"th"* words – *these, them, those, there.* I had to speak those words into a tape recorder. The thing that stands out most about speech therapy is that I bit my tongue a lot.

Left to right: Fred – aged 3, Michael – aged 4 and Paul – aged 2

Soraya Vianne George
My youngest sister and child of Ngaire and John George.
She has a husband and four children.

Mum and dad in our backyard in Clermiston Avenue, Corstorphine

Paul (aged 19) and me (aged 20) outside the front of our Macandrew Road home.

Back row standing left to right: Phillip, Michael, Paul, Mum, Dad, Fred, Fran, Nora, Peter.
Front row left to right: Neville, Soraya, Paulette, Lloma, Stephan. Myra is the only one missing.

Left to right: Paul, Neville (front), Michael, Phillip, Dad (Mr. George), Stephan, Peter and Fred taken in Macandrew Road. I was about 20 at the time (in the background is the former horse stable where I had an apartment for a few months).

Chapter Five

Boys Will Be Boys . . . Apparently

I started school at age seven. We were Roman Catholics, and religion was important in my family, but for some reason I attended first grade at a public school in Corstorphine, a suburb of Dunedin. This was regarded as a Protestant school, but there were other Catholic children attending there. Actually, the only time the Catholic-vs-Protestant thing came up was when we said the Lord's Prayer, at the start of every school day. And that's only because the Catholics say the ending differently. My teacher, Mr. Faye (also a Catholic), came up to me early on and whispered, "You don't have to say the last part of the Our Father, Fred." Which made no sense at all, it just shows you how narrow- minded people were back then.

Me, aged 7 – St Peter Chanel school photo

Me, aged 14 – taken in Corstorphine just before we moved to Macandrew Road

Michael, Brian Bridges, Paul and Dad (me in front)

Below: The St Peter Chanel School

Sometime in first grade I got a nickname. There was a cartoon character named Freddy the Frog. Because my name is Fred, some of the other kids started calling me Freddy the Frog, and saying things like, "Hey, Freddy, have you had any tadpoles lately?" I knew they were teasing but I really hated it. And, of course, they could see that I got really mad. At that time, when I got mad, I would bite my left hand to keep from striking out at somebody. I bit my hand so hard there were teeth marks all over it. So the more they teased, the more I bit my hand. And the more I bit my hand, the more they teased. It went on for a long time. I'm kind of surprised I *have* a left hand left!

Actually, now that I come to think about it, the other boys had nicknames, too. They just didn't seem to mind. My brother Peter was called Pumpkin Eater (as in, "had a wife and couldn't keep her"). Paul was called Boulos, which is Arabic for Paul. Michael was nicknamed Niger, because whenever he played sports -- especially rugby -- he would get dirty. And then there was Phil the Pill, Stephan the Heathen, and Neville the handsome devil.

We had this "uncle" Cyril who came from England. He was the brother-in-law of Lord Macintosh. He had been a prisoner of war in World War II and had suffered a lot at the hands of the Japanese. He was fed on cabbage and rice day and night. If we ever mentioned to him that we were having cabbage and rice for dinner he would hit the roof! He was an alcoholic and always had bruises on his forehead from falling. My mother was the only one who had the patience to tolerate him. I remember more than one occasion when Mum was literally carrying him into our room and as she placed him on the bottom bunk where we slept he was saying to her in a drunken tone *"Marry me, Mrs. George."* He worked at the factory in Dunedin that was owned by his brother-in-law so no matter what he did he would always have a job there.

Uncle Cyril would give us boys these delicious toffees. We would each get a different flavored one so we would take turns at sucking them. Michael would end up eating his as well as Paul's and mine so we'd all get mad at him. Eventually Cyril was confined to a wheelchair and on a Saturday I would push him to the T.A.B. to place a bet on the horses. We argued a lot. His sister would send him The London Illustrated every month which had a glossy colored front page, the only one I ever saw at the time. Eventually Cyril became too much so Mum placed him in a nursing home where he died. My mother and sisters were left what he had. My mother used her share to set up a trust fund for Soraya, the youngest member of the George family.

By the time I was in second grade, a new Catholic elementary school was being built – Saint Peter Chanel School. Most of the Catholic children transferred to this school. It was a couple of miles from where we lived but we found ways to have fun going and coming to school. We had to be innovative about having fun, because we didn't have two cents to rub together, and everything we played or played with had to be free.

There was a farm between our house and the school, and a dump just beyond the farm. The farm had cows, chickens, ducks, dogs, and cats – all the ordinary farm animals. And every now and then a cow would find a gap in the fence and get loose. Then another cow would get loose, and another, and so forth. They would head straight for the dump. And there would be chaos – farmers, animals, kids all running in different directions and making lots of noise. That *was* fun.

There were willows and other trees growing around the dump. Now this was important because we could make bows and arrows out of the different sticks. We would take a willow branch and notch it at both ends. Then we pulled a string from one end to the other. This was the bow. Short branches from the other trees made arrows. We had seen movies with Hopalong Cassidy and the Lone Ranger and Tonto, so we played cowboys and Indians a lot.

But we really had to behave ourselves in school. The teachers at Saint Peter Chanel were all nuns and were quite strict. But the nuns were understanding, too. For instance, for some reason, there weren't many boys in the class room when I started school. Most children are five when they start school whereas I was seven. The nuns held my brother Paul back, so I wouldn't feel like I was so far behind. Also, at lunch time they would have Paul and I come to the rectory to eat. They usually found some leftovers to share with us. Cottage pie was my favorite – it's an Irish pie with a lot of vegetables, minced meat, and thyme. This didn't seem unusual to me at the time but I now realize that the nuns knew how poor we were and must have felt sorry for us.

I didn't have too much trouble in school. I was pretty well-behaved. But there was a boy named Tony Kane who would act up in class and make me laugh. That's when I got in trouble. And that's when I found out what *strict nuns* meant. If you misbehaved, the nuns would get the ruler out and "wrap it around" your knuckles. This meant that they hit the knuckles on the back of your hand with the ruler. The rap didn't harm you or break anything but sure did hurt. From St Peter Chanel I would go to St Pat's next to the Catholic Church we attended.

I then went to the Christian Brothers High School. The teacher who impressed me the most was Brother Michael Frost. He was quite unassuming and would blush a lot but was a great teacher. A friend told me he used to teach math at Otago University. About a year after I quit school I learned that he had fallen off the cliffs at St Clair and died. I was shocked and saddened to hear that news.

The Brothers got a lot of respect and the classroom was very quiet but when a lay teacher called Mr. Brown came in to teach all holy hell would break loose.

Once we were out of school for the day, we ran around a lot. We had a tremendous amount of energy, and there were a lot of us, so we played games with toys we made, like the bows and arrows. When we played cowboys and Indians, we would put two clothes pegs together as a make-believe gun. We used to practice to see who had the fastest draw.

And we also played sports in the front yard. I remember that we tore the hell out of the neighbors' fences. But they were understanding because we weren't vandalizing; we were just kids roaring around and having fun. Even so, I once had a neighbor kid throw a brick at me. It was all in fun but I still had my head split open.

We used to play ball – rounder, we called it. I think this is where the concept of baseball later came from. We didn't have a ball or a bat, so we would make a ball out of rolled-up socks. Then we could usually find an old apple box or something like that, tear apart the box, and use the wood as a bat. One person would throw the tennis ball, somebody else would hit it. The idea was to catch the person and get them out, or throw the ball at the person running to a base. So every now and then you would get hit on the thigh and it would hurt like blue blazes. Or the guy who was hitting would throw the bat down, and you might get conked on the head. We were just kids, so we didn't get hurt badly and it never seemed terribly dangerous.

We used to make "trolleys" for riding down hills and racing. We sometimes called them soap box derbys, but they were a real stripped-down version of a soap box car. My older sister, Myra, had a boyfriend who was a mechanic. He would give us some old wheel bearings, about three inches in diameter, and we would use them as wheels. Then we'd attach the "wheels" to a wooden plank, lie down on it, and go tearing off down the street. There were plenty of steep grades near where we lived, so you could get going really fast. We used to race each other with these trolleys. And there were real soap box derby races in the city, which we used to get to see once in awhile.

This is the local store in Corstorphine where we went to get the bread, etc., for everyday use. It was about a mile from our house.

We would go to the golf course to earn money caddying. We went early in the morning, and we would caddy for 18 holes and earn 25 pence. Every once in a while a golfer was more generous, and that was a real treat!

Some kids, if they didn't get a caddying job, would hide in the woods off the fairway. The golfer would tee off, and if he couldn't see where the ball went, these kids would run out on the course and grab the guy's ball. Then later, they would sell it to him as a used ball. He never knew that the "used ball" he was buying was actually the same ball he had hit before and thought he had lost.

Sometimes we would walk about a mile from our house to the Freezing Works, and watch them slaughter livestock. Back then, the slaughtering wasn't as humane as it is now. Now, the animals are stunned before they are killed. But then, the cows would enter a small boxed-in area where they would be shot between the ears by a man who would then hook the carcass and hoist it up to be processed. Every so often the man who was shooting would miss, and the cow would take off down the chute into a big pit – about six feet deep and 30 feet square. Then the man would have to run around, trying to lasso the cow. We thought it was pretty exciting.

When we were real little we played in the front and back yards of our house. When we got older, we played cricket, rugby and soccer at the church school in Green Island.

The name of our rugby club was Corstorphine, and our colors were green and dark red. There was only one team but we played a lot.

We used to listen to a radio about the size of a refrigerator. The reception was so bad you had put your ear up to the speaker to hear. I remember listening to the time Neil Armstrong of the United States became the first man to set foot on the moon. I also listened in the time Peter Snell of New Zealand won the gold medal in the Olympics in the mile. Snell came from way back in the field to overcome the leader and win. You felt like you where there, it was so exciting.

We used to watch Robin Tait practice the discus throw or the shot-put on the field in Corstorphine. He was one of the most famous New Zealand athletes. He competed in the 1972 Olympics, and the stadium in Auckland was named after him (*years later when I was living in the United States, I went to a gym that was owned by a guy named Bob Backus. As we got to know each other, I learned that Bob had competed against Robin Tait in 1972. There's the "small world" department, again.*)

Around this time a family by the name of Coutts lived across the road from us. Years later a man named Russell Coutts would be the most renowned skipper in Sailing World Today. He helped win the America's Cup for New Zealand. Later he would take it away from New Zealand representing Switzerland, the current holder of America's Cup Alingri.

I also used to watch Tubby Diack work out. He'd be jogging in Corstorphine and the sweat would just pour off him. It was awesome. Tubby is not as generally well-known as Robin Tait but he played rugby for the Province of Otago, but due to an injury did not plat for The New Zealand All Blacks. And they were always the most feared and respected rugby side in the world at that time and still are.

Rugby was a big thing for us. We idolized the famous players, imitated the older players, and busted our butts when we were young in order to become good players.

It may not sound like it, but life wasn't all rugby. There was a golf course there, too, where we caddied when we were older. Corstorphine was a beautiful spot – not exactly primitive, but isolated. The ocean wasn't too far away from where we played. And there was a place called Tunnel Beach. The guidebooks all say that a man named Edward Cargill had cut a tunnel through the sandstone cliffs so his family could get down to the beach. But then I also heard that Tunnel Beach got its name from a shipwreck. When the ship had run aground there, the people on board didn't know that there was a beach close by, so they dug a tunnel to get to the land they could see. I can't really vouch for either version.

Tunnel Beach is a scenic but scary area. It juts out into the ocean, and we used to crawl out on the neck as the waves from the ocean came slamming against the rocks below the cliff. Even getting to this place was quite a challenge. There was a woman who loaded her rifle with salt pellets and shot at anybody crossing over her property. There were frog ponds and mushroom beds -- quite an adventurous trip!

Not all of our "games" were innocent, though. We also played mischievous tricks, and even got into petty theft. We would go to a small market store at the bottom of Cavasham hill. The hill was really steep, and

I used to fly down it, riding on the crossbar of my brother Michael's bicycle. It was quite exciting but dangerous.

The market store was really just a small tobacconist shop which sold candy, newspapers and cigarettes. Three or four of us would hide outside, while one of us went in and asked for something we knew they didn't have. The girl behind the counter would say, "I'll go out back and look for it. Wait just a minute." Then while she was gone, the other kids would come in the store and we would all grab handfuls of candy and run away. We did this a number of times. Everybody thought the girl was naïve, but I wound up thinking she knew about it all the time and just felt sorry for us. She never called anybody to get us in trouble.

Mr. Sidey was then the Mayor of Dunedin. His house was surrounded by huge trees, and it was kind of overhung and dark a lot. The older kids told us that Mr. Sidey had man-eating dogs that guarded his property. So, of course, we were terrified. And, of course, we dared each other to go on the property. But we were never caught – by Mr. Sidey or his man-eating dogs. Today his house is still there but there are other houses surrounding it, so I finally got to look at it

Some kids would steal milk bottle money. People in the neighborhood who had milk delivered would put the empty bottles on their porches. They would put the money for the next day's milk in one of the bottles. And this is what some kids took.

I didn't take milk money but one day we did steal lemonade bottles and got caught! We skipped school that day and were walking around the neighborhood, looking for something to do. We noticed that one house had some empty lemonade bottles on the porch.

The N.Z. All Blacks flag.
The team every rugby country side in the world wants to beat but most of the time come up short. N.Z. will host the 2011 World Rugby Cup after being denied by Australia to co-host the 2003 World Rugby Cup as they wanted it for themselves. Australia voted against N.Z.. I must say they did a good job.

The new stadium in Cardiff (with a retractable roof the only one in Europe) which hosted the World Rugby Cup 1999 which my son Adam and I went to see.
The previous one was Cardiff Arms. I had been there in 1972 when our All Blacks played Cardiff, the wooden Stadium was literally rocking as the crowd were singing Welsh songs. Sadly to say for them the mighty All Blacks won.

At this time you got money for every lemonade bottle you returned. So we ran up on the porch, grabbed the bottles, shoved them under our sweaters, and took off. The woman must have heard us because she came to the door and looked out.

We ran to hide behind the car that was parked next door. The woman didn't see us and went back into her house. But when we got up to leave, we saw that there was a boy in the window of the next-door house who had seen everything. I knocked on the window, and said, "Do you mind if we take the bottles?" He kind of shook his head, but after we were gone he must have told his mother – who told the neighbor, who called the police. And, of course, they blamed me.

We ended up going to children's court but only got a warning. The court and the policemen made an impression on me; the warning didn't. I must have been eight- or nine-years-old. I learned my lesson then from Mr. Crawford, the local policeman for our area. He had gotten authority from all the parents in the neighborhood to discipline any kid who did something real bad. And so Mr. Crawford would put the bad kid over his desk and hit him with a leather strap. Once that had happened to you, you were more careful about not getting caught doing something real bad.

When I was about ten-years-old, my brothers and I began to "smoke." We took dried leaves and the stuffing out of pillows and rolled them into newspapers. No wonder I gave up smoking when I was 12!

Unfortunately, for my brothers, they continued to smoke.

When I was about 14-years-old Paul and I were on our way home from school (C.B.H.S.) when we decided to have a look in Woolworths on Main Street in Dunedin. Unknown to me Paul was shoplifting. All of a sudden the store detective yelled out to Paul. Paul took off and I ran after him not realizing he was being pursued. The detective caught up and grabbed us both. We were taken to the manager's office. I was stunned. Fortunately he gave us a warning and told us he did not want to see us in the store again. Of course, I was innocent but guilty by association. Ironically, I would work in the same store years later. I had been working as a produce manager at the Woolworths store in Mosgiel, about eight miles from Dunedin. One day the store manager came up to me and said "I am going to give you two weeks notice" and paid me in advance. I said "so long" and went into the city and got a job in the warehouse of the Woolworths store in Dunedin (the same one that Paul had been caught shoplifting in when we were children). So I got paid from both stores at the same time for two weeks.

We also used to try to sneak into Carisbrook Stadium. This was where the big rugby and cricket matches were played. If we didn't have the money to buy a ticket, or a pass to get in . . . well, we didn't want to miss any of the games just because of that.

There was one day where we tried sneaking in and wound up with a total disaster. We didn't get caught (exactly) but it was still a total disaster. There were four of us – my brothers Michael and Paul, a friend named Brian Bridges, and me. We climbed a fence, only to discover that there was barbed wire at the top. So to avoid the barbed wire, we just jumped over it, simultaneously, thinking we would land on the ground on the other side. What we landed in was a pile of manure and grass clippings that the maintenance crew had dumped in the corner of the ground during the previous week. What a mess! We stunk to high heaven! You can bet our mothers were not too happy to see us that day, when we went home. And you can bet they told us about it, too!

To get "pocket money" we sold hot pies and candy run by a man named Don Dennis who ruled with an iron fist, at Carisbrook (the same place where we landed in the manure). We sold raffle tickets by going door to door in Kew and Corstorphine to make a few bob. We also sold beer and lemonade bottles to Mr. Ratley, the rag bone man. Mr. Ratley reminded you of the sitcom character on Steptoe & Son (English TV) and Sanford & Son (U.S. TV)

I also delivered the Evening Star and magazines to customers who ordered them. The Evening Star was the afternoon paper in Dunedin and the Otago Daily Times (the oldest paper in New Zealand) was the morning paper. The Times is now the only paper in Dunedin and just so happens to be in the same building as The Evening Star. I sold the Evening Star at night. We would be picked up by a truck and dropped off with a pile of newspapers at different corners of the city and we would yell *"Extra, extra, read all about it"* just like in the movies. Some corners were hotter sales spots than others. I also delivered The Evening Star near our house on Macandrew Road and would pick up the subscription money up for it on Saturday morning.

On a Saturday night I would go to the hospital or bars and sell the Star Sports. The patients often gave me fruit as a tip.

I also sold souvenirs such as badges and pon poms whenever there was a big rugby match at Carisbrook. I would go into a pub and a drunk would say *"what do you want sonny?"* and I would ask him nervously if he wanted a souvenir of the All Blacks or the visiting country. He would either say *"Get out of my sight"* or he would throw me some dollars and tell me to keep the change. You never knew what to expect. Out of all the transactions we would earn 20% of what we sold plus tips.

One day, I was delivering telegrams from the Post Office when I was about to go down Pit Street - heading towards Frederick and George Street. It was a steep hill. Suddenly the main bar that holds the bike together fell off and the bike collapsed. Yet another narrow escape. A guy I worked with joked that I had the fastest time for delivering a telegram as well as the slowest.

Another story involves this girl I knew who was so amused by watching me eat a Boston bun (unheard of in Boston, Mass.) that she would buy one for me with the cream oozing out the sides. Everyone got a kick out of it.

Boston buns were nine inches in diameter and so delicious, with icing and coconut on top, raisins in the dough and butter or cream in the center.

When we lived on Macandrew Road my younger brothers and I would race around the house on our bikes to see who had the fastest time. Each time one of us would knock a second off the lap time. That was a lot of fun.

Paul, Michael and I would race from our house to the nearest telephone box (about 50 yards). I would always finish third. But as mum would say one person cannot be good at everything. I would find out later in the Army that I had stamina but not speed. In the Army I took up long-distance running, an interest that would lead to me running in marathons.

I would take the bikes apart and try to put them together again, much to the mystery of my brother Peter.

One time I was riding my bicycle home from delivering the Otago Daily Times. It was early in the morning and there was a heavy frost. I must have been about 200 yards from my house when I started to feel as though I was going to faint so I pulled over to the curb and fell flat on my face into pea stones next to the side walk. I woke up in my own bed and was told that the milkman had picked me up and taken me home.

A couple moved into the house next door to us on Macandrew Road. The husband was a nephew of one the first men to climb Mount Everest – Sir Edmond Hillary of New Zealand (his guide, Nording Tanzing, was the other man). On the other side of us was another couple – the Harris's. The wife was the sister of Murry Halberg, a middle distance runner who had won a medal in the Olympics with a handicap. He also trained the great miler Peter Snell and other Olympians.

We would get up early in the morning to listen to the New Zealand rugby or cricket team who were playing there games in Europe and the West Indies, even though the reception was terrible and hard to understand. Another memory I have about my younger brothers is that they were notorious for lying in bed when they should have been getting ready for work. I would often get a facecloth and run it under the cold water. Besides getting called all the names under the sun it sure woke them up.

I have identical twin brothers, Peter and Phillip. They had a lot of fun growing up as the girls they went out with didn't know who they were going out with. I could tell the difference between them by the shape of Peter's face as it was a little rounder from eating too many pumpkins (just kidding).

I admired my sister Nora who would give all her siblings a Christmas present. It was something small from Woolworths which was all she could afford. My sister Myra worked at the movie theatre as an usherette. She let me in to see this movie "Never on a Sunday." I was about 15 and naïve. There were a lot of sexual innuendos that I did not pick up on. Myra was good to me in that respect – she would get me into the movies for free. Later on I would work at the movie theatres selling ice cream and candy. If it was a hot night the ice cream would melt before you sold it.

Front row; Soraya, Neville, Paulette, and Lloma,
Back row; Phillip, Peter, Nora, Paul and Myra

Missing Stephan, Fran, Michael, Frederick (or Jim Churchman)

I got to know Nora's and Lloma's children quite well as I babysat them a lot and also lived with Nora for a while. They were all great kids to look after. One time I was sleep walking in the middle of the night and they told me later that I tried to get into my older sister Fran's bed with whom I had a contentious relation with. That was embarrassing and funny.

I taught Paulette to drive a car. I guess I had more patience than Michael. Michael tried to teach me how to drive in my Humber Hawk. Everything went well until we turned into the driveway on Macandrew Road. When Michael said "stop" I accidentally put my foot on the accelerator. Michael grabbed the steering wheel and we missed the house by inches. After that I was taught by a professional.

Neville took me to hospital when I got injured playing rugby. I also took Neville up to Auckland with me to see Phillip who lived there. Later on I would also live there with him in Northcote, Auckland with the McConnachie's who were friends of Phillip from Dunedin.

I used to drive a truck around Dunedin. One day I was doing a delivery out to Mosgiel which is about ten miles from Dunedin. I decided to pick up Neville for company and because I thought he would enjoy the trip. I didn't know that this was against company policy. When I returned the foreman fired me. Someone must have seen Neville in the truck and ratted on me.

Paul had a reputation for getting into all kinds of trouble. It had a lot to do with the people he was associated with but he had a heart of gold. One incident I will never forget took place in Dunedin Harbour where Paul worked on a ship. On this day Paul was taking me to his ship to show me around. We were walking towards it when we heard a commotion.

A bunch of people were yelling *"throw him a lifesaver."* There were two drunken Norwegian sailors in the water. It turns out that after drinking a bottle of Ouzo each they decided to take a dip in the harbour and had jumped off their ship. One was struggling. Without hesitation, Paul threw off his jacket, ran to the side and dived in. He pulled the guy over to the barge and yanked him out of the water. Although Paul had saved his life the sailor was flailing his arms at Paul. I guess he panicked. Paul did not want any recognition but I called up the Evening Star and the next day he was on the front page of the newspaper.

I had played rugby since I was a kid. It was what everyone did when we weren't in school, and we could play outside. I had migraine headaches when I was younger, so I did not participate in organized sports.

At age 16 with my headaches cured, I joined the Dunedin Rugby Club. The picture below is the Dunedin "Under 17 Team" of 1963. We won the competition that year. We were playing for the Johnny George Memorial Trophy. Johnny George, my second cousin, was killed

UNDER 17 TEAM 1963
Winners: O.R.F.U. Championship Shield and George Shield

when he was 17-years-old in an accident at the Hillside Railways workshop. Liquid metal had spilled and poured over him. He was horribly burned, with no chance of recovery. His father Bert – my dad's cousin – dedicated the trophy to Johnny. That is how Bertie George was able to purchase The Prince Of Wales hotel from his late

son's insurance money. Also in the picture are Tommy Williams, our coach, and the late Joe Michael, another George cousin and Tommy's assistant coach.

My George brothers -- Michael, Paul, Phillip, Peter -- and I would play rugby league (similar to rugby only there are 13 players on a rugby league side whereas with rugby union there are 15). I played on the same side for Celtics in the Oval. We would get our names in the newspapers a few times. Practically half the team were "Georges." We had a tense rivalry against Kia Toa to see who had the best league side in Dunedin. Also, later on, I would follow the Boston Celtics who were a dynasty in the N.B.A. about the same time.

There were quite a few clubs then. Each club had five or six different rugby teams, at what they called grade levels. The teams in one club played each other, and they also played teams on their same level, from different clubs. For instance, the Dunedin 1st grade would play the 1st grade team from another club. It was terrific fun -- and good practice, too. You paid a membership fee to join the club, and then you accumulated points for wins, ties, and losses. Each club had its own facility, its own jerseys, its own colors, and its own grounds. It's not just a sand lot situation but instead was very well organized.

Our coach, Tommy Williams, was Lebanese and married Margaret Farry from a well known Lebanese family and the whole team was invited to the wedding which was a nice gesture. He played for the province of Otago (that's quite an achievement, in case you don't follow rugby in New Zealand). He came quite close to being an All-Star. They still tell the story of the time he played most of a game with a couple of broken ribs. He was extremely tough, a tremendous player, and a really nice guy. Well, anyway, Tommy Williams was the coach of the Dunedin Club, under 17 1/2, and he taught us a lot and helped us win the rugby competition for our level the year I was 16.

I also played rugby in a competition on Sundays for the Railways on Kettle Park (Dunedin's club grounds). We played against the Fire Department and the Police. As it was a public job we worked odd hours so most of the guys were not able to play on Saturdays like the rest of the public. My brother-in-law, John Everson, played for the Fire Department as he was an officer for them; I used to play against him.

Chapter Six

The First Doubts

I have wondered over the last three years what kind of a person I would have been if the switch at birth hadn't taken place? I have wondered how, and if, I would have been different. What things would have happened in my life that didn't. And which of the events that have occurred would not have occurred. It's really a fruitless exercise and it's not that I am full of regrets and longings. But still . . . I wonder.

I used to have these ugly duck-type feelings of being in another world, or in someone else's identity, or just not feeling normal. Actually I *was* in someone else's world, and so was Jim Churchman – he was in my world and I was in his world. I had these odd feelings, even though we did not know why at the time. And I kept trying to "be myself" – whatever that meant. My mother used to say to me, "You live in your own world." She was right. I did. I was a swan living like a swan in a world of ducklings.

My relationship with my father, John George, was difficult, cool, and distant. It gradually got better as we both grew older. And after the terrible accident he was in the year after my mother's death in 1970, we became quite a bit closer. I was always quite close to my mother and to my brothers and sisters, but my dad was another story.

There was a problem right from the beginning. When I was brought home from the hospital, he started accusing my mother of having had an affair. He said I didn't look like the rest of the family. I sure didn't look Lebanese.

I remember the times my mother reported our bad behavior to dad when he came home from work. Once, in particular, whatever was wrong involved Michael, Paul, and I. He came into the bedroom and yelled at them but never said a word to me. He never got mad at me. And I know it was not due to a lack of misbehavior on my part.

One year at Christmas time, my mother suggested that I buy him a Christmas present. When I handed him my present dad just looked at me and said, "Why would you want to buy *me* a present?"

Front row; Stephan & Peter
Back Row; Phillip, Michael, Neville, Paul - missing are the two guys that were switched at birth - Frederick John George and James Francis Churchman.

These are the guys that I used to get into mischief with e.g. we would go to the beach which was a few miles from our house and raid orchards on the way, in fact we named the large apples after Stephan - we would call them "Stephan's head" as he had a small head, we would jump on each other's shoulders to reach the apples.

But there were other, happier memories, too. The Cedar Club was the Lebanese club in town, the place where they had parties and played cards and bingo. Even though my father did not drink, he could be very entertaining at times. At wedding receptions he was the life of the party. He loved to get up and dance. Or he would get up on a chair, make a monkey face, and say, "Where are my bananas?" That never failed to bring the house down with laughter. One of my father's favorite lines was that when he got married "all I had was my false teeth and a toothbrush." Another of his standing jokes was about the kid who wanted to go to the orphanage picnic so bad that he shot his parents.

Then again, Father used to talk angrily about religion and praised the other, richer Lebanese, but he always seemed to be able to have more fun than anybody else – especially the rich ones who counted on their dignity to be liked.

Sometimes when I went to see him at the Cedar Club he would be playing cards with other Lebanese men and would look up at me and be so happy to see me. At those special times I would really feel like his son. It was a whole different world.

Dad and I used to place bets on the horses together. And there was a horse named Frederick. We bet on him together, and he won a few races. We had a lot of laughs over that, and it brought us closer.

Still, we often argued with each other. We argued about religion a lot, and he would say things like, "What do *you* care what I think?" Once I really made him mad when I yelled at him and said, "So why did you give Mum so many kids?" I already knew the answer to that –because the church wouldn't allow people to use birth control. He retaliated by saying, "What, do you want me to give Soraya back? You're not my son."

Dad must have known that there had been a mix up. My mother would always console me, and tell me she understood and that, of course, I was his son. I was quite close to my mother. She was always extremely supportive and encouraging, especially when I first went to look for a job. She was always right there with me. I remember some of the things she said to me, and they still touch and inspire me.

Because of my mother's loyalty, love and support, I would try to help her all I could. I helped her with the laundry, for instance. What a production! There were two laundry tubs, great big round galvanized tubs on legs. One of them had a scrubbing board in it and other a wringer. There also was a covered copper tub that had a fire underneath it. This was how we got the hot water.

First we'd put a batch of clothes – or diapers, there were always lots of diapers – in the first tub which had warm water and some soap. We'd let the wet things soak for a little while, and then start scrubbing whatever hadn't come clean by soaking. Then we would run the clean pieces through the wringer – two rollers, turned by a hand crank – and into the cold rinse water. From there, the clothes would go through the wringer again, and get hung outside on the clothes line. Then we'd start praying that it wouldn't rain. If it rained, all the laundry had to be dried in the house.

One time I was riding a horse around our back yard. Apparently I was sitting too far back, too close to his rump. Somehow he got spooked, and bolted. When he ran under the clothes line, I was knocked off his back and was nearly choked by the clothes line. It was a long time before I got up enough courage again to ride a horse. But I'm not sure which I regretted most – falling off the horse, or having to do the laundry all over again.

I would help Mum clean the house on Saturday morning. It wasn't a big house, but with 15 people running around in it, cleaning was a big job. She would pay me when she could – five shillings, which was a lot of money then. But I helped her whether she paid me or not. We couldn't afford to hire any help, and although it was tough to bring up that size a family, there were other families nearby who had as many children, and no more money than we did.

There was no TV when I was little, and when there was most folks couldn't afford to buy one so they rented it by the week. Practically everybody had a coal stove in the kitchen, though. It served a lot of different functions: Not only did you cook on it, it provided heat for the kitchen, and it also heated the hot water tank which was right beside it. Most everybody spent a lot of time in the kitchen, especially on a cold day.

When we lived in Corstorphine, we had a meter for electricity. You would put one shilling at a time in the meter. And if you were heating a lot of water, it would only last about half an hour. So you always kept a lot of coins around.

Nobody had a washing machine or refrigerator. I remember that we kept the butter in a wire mesh box that protruded outside the house to keep it cool.

We ate a lot of bread. I remember buying ten loaves of fresh-baked bread from the nearby bakery on Friday morning. The bread would be gone by Saturday night, and Mum would have to bake scones for Sunday, because the baking company did not bake bread on weekends. We had wonderful-tasting things to put on the bread: butter, golden syrup, all kinds of jams, peanut butter, and honey. We even put vegemite, which is black-colored and has a strong taste, on fresh Italian bread with butter and lettuce. It was out-of-this-world delicious.

My mother and sisters were quite resourceful as they made there own dresses cut out of patterns on a sewing machine and Mum would mend our socks with a light bulb inserted inside the sock. With a needle and thread, she would also patch our trousers if they needed it.

The Lebanese brought their culture and customs to New Zealand. But when it came to cooking not all of the traditional Lebanese ingredients were available so they had to improvise. We ate a lot of rice, prepared in a lot of different ways. Mum also made huge pots of vegetable soup, cooked for a long time with a bone in it to give it flavor.

Every Tuesday there was an auction in the city, where you could buy grain, fruit, and vegetables in big sacks and crates. They were a lot cheaper than you could get them in the market. Dad used to get a van and go to the auction. Then he would bring the food back, sell it to the neighbors in smaller quantities, and make a small profit. And we got food that way which we couldn't have afforded to buy at the market. He would buy sacks of potatoes and rice which would last a long time.

We also had a small garden in the back yard. We grew potatoes, I remember. We used to peel the potatoes, light a fire, melt some lard in a tin can, put the cut-up potatoes in it and, presto!, French fries. We also had radishes, cabbage, rhubarb, beans, parsley and strawberries.

In the fall, some of the neighbors had apple trees growing in their yards, and the branches would hang over the sidewalks. We would walk along there and jump on each other's shoulders and grab all the apples we could.

We also had kiwi fruit, before it became commercially available anywhere else. We called them Chinese gooseberries, and were they luscious! I still love kiwis, and I'm really glad that the New Zealanders started exporting them in the mid-1970s. Otherwise, I might have to do without them now that I live in Massachusetts.

Well, anyway, we ate pretty well.

My dad worked steady. It was hard to support such a big family, and he couldn't afford to be out of a job. He drove trucks, took laboring jobs and cut hair but mostly worked at meat packing plants, slaughter houses, and butcher shops. Butcher shops were like 7-11's today; they were everywhere. People didn't have refrigerators, let alone freezers, and they purchased food on a day-to-day basis. So no matter what area, city, or town – you could always find a butcher shop. New Zealand is an agricultural country, so there were plenty of sheep and cattle. And my dad could always find a job. The slaughterhouse was seasonal work and lasted for about eight months of the year. Dad would spend the remaining four months cutting hair for a living.

My mother worked when she could, too – when she was between babies. She once worked cleaning commercial property and as a waitress in a number of different cafes – the Continental, the Little Hut. She often went to Godfrey's Bakery (the bakery I would work at years later when I was 18). She would occasionally get stale bread from the bakery, mix it with milk, sugar, eggs, cinnamon, vanilla and raisins and wind up with bread pudding. That was really good. I love bread pudding to this day, and I would make it when there was nothing else to eat when I was growing up in Corstorphine. When we have stale bread that is when I have the impulse to make bread pudding. One time I remember there was a loaf of bread between ten of us and nothing else in the house but we found a way of surviving tough times. You learnt to accept what you had and what you did not have.

Sometimes – and this was a rare treat -- Mum would get cream buns for us – these are regular buns, with raspberry jam and whipped cream inside. We loved the cream buns even more than the bread pudding – probably because we didn't have them often.

There was an organization in New Zealand called the Dunkley Society founded by a very wealthy man that was actually a network of foster homes. It was designed to offer care – in a foster home – for the children of pregnant women who could not afford to get their other children taken care of while the new baby was being born. Because the foster homes were just regular homes, not institutions, a mother could do this and not have to worry about her older children while she herself was in a maternity home. It was really a great deal. I stayed in a Dunkley Home a couple of times.

The first time, I went to a town called Pleasant Valley in Palmeston, about 30 miles from Dunedin. I had to take a train to get there, and I can remember Mum putting me on the train. The young couple who owned the farm where I stayed was quite nice to me, and helped me. I remember a few things from that time. I taught myself how to ride a bicycle. There were sheep and cattle and a sawmill on the farm.

There was another boy there, a kid with real problems! He was obnoxious and aggressive, and really annoyed me. He pulled my hair and wouldn't back off so I finally got mad and dropped him. That caused some trouble, but finally the couple we were staying with understood that I wasn't the one to blame, and everything was then okay.

One time we went to the Waverly Boy's Home, not a Dunkley home but an institution run by the nuns. It was awful. We used to say that it was almost like being in a concentration camp. I can still smell the polish from the floors. The nuns were really insistent about having the floor polished. We would have rags soaked with polish on our feet, and kind of skate along the floors – polishing, always polishing.

I also went to another home that was south of Dunedin, in a suburb called Anderson's Bay. And, as I discovered many years later, this was where the Somervilles – my birth mother's family – settled. The original Somerville house is still there, just up from Somerville Street (which is, of course, named after them). This is one of the many kind of weird "coincidences" that has happened over and over again.

Long before I knew of my connection with the Churchman/Somerville family, they touched my life in strange, almost indirect ways. Many years later, I worked as an adult apprentice for a builder and my job was working on a house in this very area. The same builder built the Garden Tavern, which was owned by the Lebanese, which I also worked on.

Taken at St. Kilda beach in Dunedin.
Left to right: Phillip, Fred, American Sailor (Nora's friend) and Michael

Being underprivileged kids (Dunkley society) we were invited to have ice cream and jelly and candy whenever a U.S. Frigate was in port on its way to the Antarctica

At this same time, my brother Michael (who was a year older than I was) had been sent to a Dunkley Home about 100 miles north of Dunedin, in a town called Timaru. Timaru is a town about a quarter the size of Dunedin, probably about 30,000 people. Michael started attending public school there, and he made friends with a guy named Jim Churchman. This was the first time any of us had met any of the Churchmans. We didn't then know anything about them, or that there was any connection between our families.

Gordon Churchman was a school principal, and frequently got transferred from school to school. The

Churchman family, having been in Dunedin when Jim was born (and when the switch was made), was in Timaru when Michael was there.

Michael was fostered out to Cedric Leeming's house in Timaru. He was sent to the Timaru Boys Technical High School for a semester. It was at school where he met Jim Churchman (my switch) and became friends with him. He nicknamed Jim "church mouse" which stuck with him.

Gordon Churchman was transferred back to Dunedin as principal of the elementary school where the original Somerville homestead is in Anderson's Bay. The Churchman family lived in the northern part of the city, and we lived in South Dunedin. I didn't meet any of them at this time.

(Another coincidence. Simon Leeming, who lives in Canterbury, New Hampshire, is my lawyer and is the Honorary Consulate of New England for New Zealanders. Simon is the nephew of Cedric Leeming – the man who fostered Michael for a semester. Simon and wife Alice hold a "Maori Hangi" (food is cooked under the ground) once a year for about 500 ex-pats, including me.)

My late brother Michael and his wife Lynda.

I was best man at their wedding. I had to read out the telegrams, but because I was so nervous and my sister Nora was laughing in the front row I froze and Michael grabbed the telegrams and read them himself.

Michael met his brother, Jim Churchman, when he was a teenager in a town 100 miles from where we were born. They became good friends but sadly Michael passed away without knowing that Jim was his brother.

Jim and Michael remained good friends. And Jim hung around our house in his youth. At this point, my mother started to get suspicious because Jim looked so much like my brothers and sisters. He's a little taller, but otherwise he looked to be 100% George, plus he had Mum's rosy cheeks. Jim also was known as something of a daredevil (a George trait), while I was more conservative (a Churchman trait). Mum found out that Jim had been born in the same hospital almost at the same time as I was after talking to Jim. Jim had commented to Mum how much I looked like his family, especially his brother Owen. Mum must have thought to herself that my birthday was on Dec. 22 (another mistake, more about that later) while Jim's birthday was on Dec. 24 (my real birthday). I'm sure Mum thought, "How can that be, there's more than a day between the two birthdays). She started to suspect the truth at this time, but there was no DNA to uncover the secret. But, bless her, she said to herself, "I am not about to give Fred up after all these years."

Jim was sufficiently concerned that he talked to his father and asked that Gordon Churchman check things out with the family doctor. Of course the doctor is the last one who would either know or admit to knowing if a mistake had actually been made. Also, there really wasn't any sure-fire way to verify anything at this point. There were no hand prints or footprints on the hospital records, and DNA technology would not be available until the 1980s.

The Churchman family (minus me). See how much Jim sticks out – it is quite obvious that he is a 'George'.

At any rate, the doctor told Mr. Churchman, "Gordon, he's your son. No question about it, he's your son." And Mr. Churchman told Jim the same thing: "You're my son without question. And I don't want to hear anything more about this."

Left: Gordon Churchman's summer cottage (my birth father).

Coincidently Mrs. George (mum) had a friend that had a cottage further down the road near the beach; we used to go there in the summer. Also, my late brother Michael and his wife Glynnis would live in the same small town about 26 miles from the city of Dunedin.

Right: This saucer cottage at Warrington belongs to Gordon's neighbor

Chapter Seven

Hobbies, Occupations, The Army and Altercations

The Lebanese picnic was the event of the year. We looked forward to it, and had more fun at it than you could imagine. Women would cook traditional Lebanese food for days ahead to bring to the picnic.

The picnic lasted all day and into the night, with lots of food, music, dancing, sack races, and foot races. My dad always raced and got the nickname Cheetah because he almost always won. Just before the races started, he would complain about his leg, and so would be given a head start. He'd won by the handicap they gave him plus more. We always got home after the picnic stuffed, over-fed and exhausted but ready to start looking forward to next year's picnic.

We went to the movies every Saturday morning. My brothers and I would take the bus into town, go to the Chums Club at the State Theatre, and see cowboy movies like Hopalong Cassidy or the Lone Ranger and Tonto, and cartoons like Tom and Jerry. Sometimes we even went to another movie in the afternoon. It only cost pennies, so somehow we were able to do it. We would buy fish and chips after for lunch -- it was delicious!

I liked to read comic books -- the size of the *Readers Digest*. There were war comics, funny comics, and western comics (my favorites) about Kit Carson and Buffalo Bill. The stories followed pretty much the same pattern – the good guys always killed the bad guys in the end, and rode off into the sunset with the fair young maiden – but we never noticed. We always found comic books entertaining.

We used to have what we called "swap shops." You could go in and, for a penny or two, swap your old books and comics for other ones. It was a good deal because, of course, we couldn't afford to buy all new books and comics. It worked pretty well, and somehow it seemed that everybody came out ahead – something new to read, and a few pennies in your pocket to boot. We also used to go to our friends' houses to swap comics with them – free of charge, of course.

I liked music, too, as I grew older. Not the Beatles right at first (although a lot, later on. I even have an autographed photo of Ringo Starr). But I liked the Dave Clark Five, Gene Pitney, and Dusty Springfield. I saw

Pitney and Springfield perform at the Dunedin Town Hall. I also saw Roger Whittaker perform in Boston some years later. A great entertainer, Roger Whittaker also is one of my favorites.

Madame Tussaud's Wax Museum.

In the back of photo are Charlie Chaplin and me. When we were growing up in Corstorphine as there was no T.V. it was a big thrill for us to see silent movies with him and other performers like The Keystone Cops etc. It would cost us three pence to get a bus into the city and four pence on the way back as the bus would go a different route. It cost nine pence for front row seats and four pence for an ice-cream.
When I was in my teens I would work selling candy etc. in the theatre's
The Beatles need no introduction. Paula and I have an autograph photo of Ringo Starr addressed to us, as Jessica's friend was doing musical work for him in London.

My sisters were very big on Elvis Presley, the Everly Brothers, and Buddy Holly. They had boyfriends -- local guys we called the Dingle Boys -- who wore leather jackets and sported greasy, slicked-back hair like Fonze, that cool guy from "Happy Days." The Dingle Boys had their own gangs – not criminal gangs, just a bunch of guys who hung out together.

We all went to dances on Friday nights, usually at a club in South Dunedin. We weren't too keen on ballroom dancing, but we liked the Twist, and the

Swim. I met a girl from Scotland at the dance club (little did I know then that Scotland is where my Somerville ancestors came from) and began dating her. We used to go to the movies, such as *To Sir, With Love* starring Sidney Poitier, and then to a coffee shop,

Me at a dance in my early 20s.

and then to the bus stop so she could catch her bus home to Brockville.

An odd thing happened a few years later when I first went to the Balclutha Freezing Works, looking for a job. While sitting in the lunch room with some of the guys that worked there, I noticed one of the fellows across the room looking at me. He came over to me and said, "Are you Owen Churchman's brother?" I said, "No, I'm not his brother. I don't even know Owen, but I do know Jim." The guy just looked at me kind of funny and walked off.

My brother Phillip George would be walking down the main street of Dunedin and a complete stranger would walk up to him and ask if he were Jim Churchman's brother. Innuendoes

Like that made us curious whether there was a mix-up at the hospital. Jane Churchman (my biological sister) told me Jim cautioned her when she was growing up not to get to close to the George boys!

At one stage of Gordon Churchman's career he taught at a school in the town of Balclutha south of Dunedin. In fact Jim's and Owen's wives, Marge and Janis, came from Balclutha. It made me kind of curious about meeting this Churchman family but we didn't meet because they lived in North Dunedin and we lived in South Dunedin.

My first job was at Barton's Butcher Shop, a huge place that always claimed to be the biggest butcher shop in the southern hemisphere. They did everything there from butchering to processing. They even took the fleece from the sheep, dyed the wool, and sold it. The original owner, George Barton, went to the stockyards every Tuesday and personally selected the cattle they purchased. The cattle were slaughtered at the abattoirs. Some of the meat was sold fresh, some was frozen, and some was processed. They made sausages, roast beef, wiener schnitzel, and all kinds of smoked meat.

Old George Barton was still alive when I started working there but died not long after. While buying cattle at the stockyards, he fell off one of the pens. The day of his funeral, the shop was supposed to be closed. But the old man's sons – George Jr. and Reg -- just pulled the blinds down over the windows, locked the doors, and told us to keep working. They named a horse race after him called *"The George Barton Memorial"* at Forbury race track. I was paid four and a half pounds a week. If I worked Friday night, I got five pounds. That was because Friday night was when all the floors were cleaned. We'd got down on our hands and knees and scrape the sawdust off the floors, all over the whole plant, and replaced it with new sawdust. Barton's was one of the first butcher shops to sell prepacked meat.

As soon as I got a job, I began paying for my lodging at home. I did ask Mum if I could skip the first week's board because I needed to buy a pair of dress shoes – which cost seven and a half pounds. Of course she said yes. But I never missed another payment. I stayed at Barton's for four months. It was a different place after the old man died. George Jr. asked me to stay on but I told him I wanted to get a government job. So I walked across the road, and applied at the main post office.

One of the things you needed to provide when you applied for a postal job was your birth certificate. I had brought mine, after obtaining it from the Registry. I was astonished to see that my birthday - which for 16 years I had thought was December 22nd – was, according to the birth certificate, actually on December 23rd. I kind of shrugged my shoulders, and figured it was some kind of bureaucratic snafu, and didn't think too much about it. From then on, though, I celebrated my birthday on the 23rd until I found out about the switch 40 years later. After that, my official birthday became December 24th. So that's where all those birthdays come from. It would be too complex to change my name or date of birth now so I will remain as Frederick J. George.

Anyway, I had a number of different jobs. I worked at Cadbury's chocolate factory twice, and at the Great King Car Painters. Wherever I was, though, when I got home from work Aunty Jean would have a hot meal waiting for me. She was always good to me.

Horseracing was big all over New Zealand. There was no television when we were growing up, so the races were broadcast on the radio. They would broadcast the fifth and the seventh events of the horse race. This was called "the daily double." You would think that listening to a horse race on the radio wouldn't be entertaining, but the announcers were all moonlighting – their full-time jobs were as auctioneers. So they were able to speak even better than ordinary announcers. They were extremely animated and spoke very fast (I've heard some of them say the names of six horses in one breath!), and the closer the horses came to the finish line, the faster and higher-pitched their voices became.

This is where Cardigan Bay is buried. The first pacer to win $1m back in 1973 at Alexandra Park Raceway, Auckland, NZ.

When I was in New Zealand in 1995 I went to a small town called Mataura where my sister and family live. A famous All Black, Justin Marshall, hails from Mataura as does my best friend Brent Wilson's wife, Katie. Mataura is in the Province of Southland and is where the famous racehorse Cardigan Bay (named after a place in Wales) was bred.

I interviewed the daughter, son-in-law and grandson of the original trainers and breeders of Cardigan Bay, the Todd brothers. The son-in-law told me that they did not think Cardigan Bay was going to amount to much. In fact, they had another horse (Blue Prince, a half brother of Cardigan Bay) that would beat him in trials. Cardigan Bay did not have great heritage plus he was gelded so he was no good for breeding. They entered Cardigan Bay in saddle trot races at the beginning of his career and eventually he became unbeatable in New Zealand and Australia in harness racing (pacers). He overcame many injuries and handicaps and won the New Zealand trotting cup over two miles with a handicap of 56 yards.

Mrs Deans from Auckland purchased Cardigan Bay from the Todd brothers and hired Peter T. Wolfenden, the top driver and trainer in New Zealand, to train and drive him. I interviewed Peter Wolfenden at his ranch in Auckland. My late brother, Paul, was holding the video camera. Wolfenden told me how

Cardigan Bay would overcome adversity to win many races.

Eventually he was shipped to the United States at six-years-old (which is old for a racehorse). He was purchased by a syndicate for $100,000 in US$$ on the stipulation that he spend his last days in New Zealand. Mrs. Deans had to love horses because that was a lot of money in those days.

In the States he was trained and driven by Stanley Dancer who was considered the best in the world. They had match races with a champion three-year-old racehorse called Overtrick from America, over a mile from a mobile start. There were only inches between them at the finish line and they took turns of beating each other plus breaking the world record for a mile at that time. He became the first pacer in the world to win $1 million when he was 11-years-old. I once read that a veterinarian said he had an unusually large heart which made him a champion.

There was another race horse born in Mataura called Phar Lap who won 37 of his 51 starts – one of them being the richest race in North America. Phar Lap was raised in a town outside of Timaru (where Michael became friends with Jim). There is a statue of Phar Lap in Timaru and the city also has a gas station, a street and a store named after this famous race horse.

The Aussies take credit for Phar Lap's feats because he was an offspring of an exiled horse from Australia. It was recently learned through forensics that

Phar Lap died of arsenic poisoning. It is believed the horse was administered tonics and ointments containing both arsenic and strychnine. I have seen the movie made about Phar Lap and it doesn't even mention New Zealand! There was another movie called "Gallipoli," starring Mel Gibson, about the time during Word War I when Australian and New Zealand soldiers were massacred by the Turks. Again, in the movie, there was no mention of the New Zealand soldiers, even though New Zealand suffered the most casualties per population during WWI than any other of the Allied Forces. For some reason, to many in the world New Zealand does not get the credit it deserves compared to Australia.

Most other countries where horse racing is broadcast on the radio have announcers who speak as if they were having a conversation. But in New Zealand it's like you were there on the course. The announcers made it that bright and clear and exciting. Everybody followed the horse races, and most people bet on them. And you know that people pick their favorites in really bizarre ways, and have really strange stories to tell about their winners. I did, too.

I once had a dream in which a horse named Magic Casement won at really great odds. The first thing I did when I woke up was to check the racing line-ups. The race book was not printed until the next day and as this was his first start for that meeting I had no way of knowing Magic Casement was racing at all. I guess it was a premonition. When I looked in the race book, though, there was his name. So I bet on him and, sure enough, he won by a nose! Another time – on a Friday the 13th – I was placing bets, and mistakenly put my money on the wrong horse, not the one I had intended to back. But I couldn't change the bet, so I sat back and watched. And my horse – the horse I hadn't meant to bet on – won the race. After that, even on Friday the 13th, nothing could go wrong.

I used to lend my brothers money so I kept a black book. Michael was the hardest to get the money back from as he was a bit of a con-artist and it was all a joke to him. He used to borrow my wallet to impress his girlfriend, Lynda, whom he would later marry and have three kids with. Michael and Eric George would often drive down the road towards the beach with two girls in *my* car whilst I walked to work. They would be yelling and waving at me as they drove by.

One time I bet Michael I would pay for the bets at the race track that night if he beat me to St. Clair and back. Of course he beat me as he found a short cut. Another time we got a tip on a horse Michael and I bet on (with my money, of course) down in Southland. The horse was way out in front coming around the straight, according to the commentator who was known to drink in between races. Anyway, the horse finished dead last.

Both my aunts – Aunty Jean and Aunty Margaret – were racing fans. On Fridays they would buy the racing paper, called the *Friday Flash*. It gave you all the racing information for Saturday's races such as who the jockey was, what horse he was riding, the state of the track, if the horse ran well on it, etc. They got me hooked! I enjoyed reading it; my aunts enjoyed squabbling over the information as they decided what horses to back. They loved the races, and must have placed their bets pretty well because they couldn't afford to lose much money.

I remember noticing, when I worked at the Cadbury plant two different times, that there was a printing company across the road. The name of the printing company was Coulls, Somerville and Wilkie one of the oldest and best printing works in Australasia. The Somerville name didn't mean anything to me at the time, but I remembered it. And now it turns out that I was related to that "Somerville" all the time! This is another coincidence that cropped up before I knew about the switch, but that stuck in my mind. Also I was not aware of it then but my father's (Mr. George) cousin's husband, Tony Milne, worked as a lithographic artist for 50 years at the printing plant. Another ironic twist is that my biological cousin Peter Churchman was raised a Catholic because his father converted to Catholicism after marrying his mother. Peter worked for a well-known Dunedin Lebanese lawyer, John Farry, for a few years.

After I left school, I got a little wilder. I didn't get into a lot of trouble at first, and wasn't particularly rebellious or anything, but was really into the weekends – parties, dancing, horse racing, pubs.

When I was around 17-years-old, I got a car – a Humber Hawk. I wasn't old enough to sign for it myself, so I had my dad sign. It became a joke between us – whether it was my car or his. My younger brothers somehow got a duplicate ignition key made, and when I was at the movies or at a dance or at a girl's house, they would come by and take my car. Then when I was ready to go home – no car. So I left very little gas in it. As a result, people would see my car on the side of the road, or someone pushing it, to get it to jump start. They thought that was tremendously funny. I could see the humor, too, but I don't think I ever appreciated it as much as they did.

I once had a girlfriend who lived with her mother in a tiny house and the roof was leaking. I decided I would try and fix it for her. I was up on the corrugated iron roof when all of a sudden I slid right off! Their front drive was steep and I just missed the metal handrail and went tumbling down the hill. Luckily I only had a sore knee and shoulder.

Some years before, my dad had purchased a big old station wagon – big enough so that we could all sit in the back. It actually wasn't a good deal because he split the cost with a Maori friend of his who worked with him at the Freezing Works. Their agreement was that each of them would get the car for six months. For six months my dad would have the car, and then his friend would have the car for the next six months. And so on. Well, my dad had the car for the first six months, gave it to his friend, and his friend took off. We never saw him again! So here's my dad, out half the cost of the car, with this big family, and no car. When I got the Humbar Hawk, I was the only one in the family with a car. I had it for about three years.

I was a good driver, and pretty conservative, but I had a lot of trouble with cars. I was once driving the Humber Hawk after doing a lot of mechanical work on it, including fixing the brakes. I came up on a side road to an intersection with the main road. I put my foot on the brake, and . . . nothing! And I went flying through the intersection hardly slowing down. Fortunately there were no cars coming. This is the kind of thing that has happened to me a lot.

Another time, I was driving home from work, still wearing my heavy boots. I came to an intersection, went to apply the brake, but hit the accelerator instead. It was a small car, with the two pedals pretty close together, but I think my boots were just too big. This was another incident where I went flying through an intersection, against the red light, and escaped having an accident. Either God had His arm around me, or it was just not my time to go. Or maybe both. At any rate, cats with their nine lives have nothing on me.

I still had the Humbar Hawk when I taught my brother-in-law how to drive. I didn't actually realize that he didn't *know* how to drive. He said he had driven his brother's car (his brother was a race car driver), and just needed to review the basics. So I said okay. (The front and back doors on the passenger side were tied together so you couldn't open them. I had to climb in the back seat on the driver's side). Well, it was a disaster. He rocketed around the streets, making racing changes, and going from one side of the road to the other side-swiping parked cars. Somehow we made it home and parked the car. We raced behind our house on Macandrew Road hoping that nobody had seen us. But somebody had seen us, identified the car, and called the police. When the cops came around, they threw the book at us. The resulting fines and tickets and other problems – definitely not worth it.

Then I bought a Ford Prefect which was a doomed car from the start. A relative of ours used to have parties at a hotel he owned, called The Prince of Wales. I got invited to the parties, and used to have a great time. One time in particular I had gone to a party with a friend of mine. We had met some girls and had a couple of drinks. Then, later, I was driving them home in the little Prefect. At one spot, I came to a stop sign, stopped, and then started through the intersection. All of a sudden here comes this big American car down the hill and through the intersection, without stopping or yielding. He hit us square on. My car flipped over, and we ended up on the road upside down. The windshield was smashed, and that's how we had to get out of the car – through the smashed windshield. Nobody was badly hurt, but my car was a total write-off.

Actually, the insurance company threatened not to pay because they claimed I didn't admit I had been drinking. I had to threaten to take them to court. Only then did they pay what they owed me.

One of the jobs I had before I went into the Army was delivering coal. I drove a flatbed truck, loaded with hundred-pound bags of coal. There were all different kinds of coal, and I had to deliver the right coal to the right house, unload it, and put it in the customer's coal box.

There was one time – it was actually at the same place where some years before I had started to teach my brother-in-law to drive – when I came around a corner too fast and all the coal skidded off the truck. It's all over the road, burst out of the bags, and all the different kinds of coal mixed together. What a mess!

Fortunately, the policeman who came to the scene was pretty sympathetic. He got some city workers to help shovel the coal back into the sacks, and they sent me on my way. The only problem was that the coal had been all mixed up. I didn't have any idea what type of coal should be delivered to any of the customers. This was one of the times I got fired from this job. Actually, I think I got fired about three times.

Once I got stuck going down a long, steep driveway, and the company had to come and tow me out of there. Bang! You're fired. Another time I was trying to cut corners by dragging the coal sacks across the customer's yard, instead of carrying them. I guess I must have slipped, because the next thing I knew I was flat on my back with all this coal scattered around me. You've got it – bang! You're fired.

But the foreman who kept firing me was a good guy. He would fire me one day, and then the next day would ask, "You want your job back?" It was dirty and tough work but I enjoyed it, so I kept going back. Ironically Jim Churchman also worked at the same company on Saturday mornings cutting wood but I did not have any contact with him.

Along the way, I did some things I'm not particularly proud of. I was going out with a girl from Southland who had invited me to down to her house for the weekend, and we went to the horse races. I bet more than I could afford, and lost. That set me up for drinking too much when we went to a party that night. I was drunk enough that, finding the toilet occupied and feeling that I couldn't hold it, I urinated in the bathtub. A guy started yelling at me and we began fighting. He had hit me a couple of times, but I had knocked him into the bathtub and was really starting to beat him up, when another guy – who hadn't been part of the fight until then – slugged me in the kidneys. It knocked me out and stopped the fight, but it didn't spare me the embarrassment – or the hangover - of the next morning.

Another time I had had too much to drink and not enough to eat after working a long day. I came home in a taxi, and slammed the door on the taxi (which understandably caused the driver to get bent out of shape), argued with the driver, and finally staggered into the house. In the middle of the night, when I got up to go to the bathroom, I was still so drunk that I started to urinate on the floor in the hallway. I only came to my senses (more or less) when my Dad started yelling at me.

Much later in life I worked at a shoe factory in Randolph, Mass, for a couple of months. One day this kid was screaming in my ear for some reason when I inadvertently punched him. Then this other guy jumped on my back and started to hit me with a sneaker. I found out later on it was his father. The supervisor spoke to us in the office and we shook hands. Everything was fine after that.

Another incident happened when I was working in South Boston at a foundry. Paula's Uncle Nino, who worked there, got me the job. It was a very hot place to work, especially in the summer with its extreme temperatures. One day, for some unknown reason, this African-American driving a forklift charged at me. I stepped aside and then went over, pulled him out of the cab, and we started throwing punches at each other. I tripped over the metal railing and he kicked me with his metal toe boots and knocked out my two front teeth (I didn't feel a thing). That Christmas I was singing *"all I want for Christmas is my two front teeth."* I lost my job but the company paid to have my teeth fixed.

Another skirmish which comes to mind was when a guy was picking on my younger brother Phillip. At a party one night I asked him about it. He said "I will tell you about it" and without warning threw a punch. Some guys at the party separated us. A few days later I saw him walking down the main street in Dunedin so I let him have it. We were separated by some guys nearby.

The second job I had was working at the main Post Office as a Telegraph Boy. There was a big kid who was annoying me so I "dropped him." I was just sticking up for my rights. Growing up I found myself in many situations where I would turn the other cheek instead of resorting to violence. Most of the time my ego was the only thing hurt. By not retaliating it seemed to hurt the other guy's pride more than mine. Deep down I am dead set against violence.

But in spite of these things, it didn't look like I got into a lot of trouble. Many of the teenagers in our neighbourhood were always in trouble. There were a lot of unscrupulous guys around, and they were thought to be "cool" by most of the kids my age. Because I didn't hang out with them, I didn't get into too much trouble. I know it made other people think I was boring in a way, but I always tried to stay on the straight and narrow. I think I was trying to make an impression for the good on my siblings – especially my younger brothers and sisters. I tried to help them where I could.

For instance, when I was still in school at CBHS, I had learned boxing. It cost me five shillings, and a guy named Larry Salmon was the teacher as well as the masseur for the Otago rugby team. Years later, I helped my brother Peter train. He was a good boxer. One of the things we did together was running; we would get up early every morning and run like crazy from our house in Ascot Street down into the Tahuna area and back. Peter eventually became the New Zealand amateur featherweight champion.

I didn't preach at my brothers and sisters. (Mostly I find that people, who preach at me about what not to do, wind up doing exactly those things. It's kind of a waste of time.) But I used to tell my younger brothers and sisters – and my own kids, later, "You can't like everyone and you can't expect everyone to like you. Just try to do the right thing."

Actually, maybe it was my inborn biological temperament or genetic pool that kept me out of serious trouble. The Churchmans are quiet, conservative, and unruffled. It's the Georges who are more flamboyant, devil-may-care. Being a George meant nothing fazes you, nothing bothers you; everything is a kind of a joke. I was always kind of different from that. Maybe the biology and genetics explains it all.

There was no question about going to college. We just didn't have the money. Some of the Lebanese have wealth behind them; either they were wealthy when they came to New Zealand, or they worked to accumulate money and to invest what they had. Their kids went on to college, and became doctors and lawyers. I don't mean to sound like I feel sorry for myself – it was just a fact of life.

I got a job on the railways, working on the steam locomotives. I worked there for three years and became qualified as a locomotive assistant. We had a stationary boiler in the sheds that was used for heat and hot water. As an apprentice we would maintain the boiler, make sure it had enough water on the gauge and shovel coal into the fire box when needed. The boiler had to be maintained around the clock, so we took turns working on it. There was one guy, whose nickname was "Hitler," who would leave the place in a mess. I would fight with him every time I changed shifts with him; it was stressful coming into work knowing he was on duty.

Another of our duties was to light the steam engines on Sunday to get prepared for the upcoming work week. We would throw huge logs of wood in the fire box, add oily rags, then light newspaper on the end of a stick, throw it in and off it went. Later, after the fire got going, we would add coal to get the temperature up to 180 degrees f. to create steam to get the engine going, resulting in a lot of noise, hissing and puffing. The drivers would come out with there oil cans and lubricate all the moving parts, check the brakes and make sure there was enough sand for the brakes to work safely.

I had a close call when I went to pull the lever over to change the tracks for the shunt engine. The driver put the brakes on because the tracks were wet as it was raining. As I was about to run over the track, I hesitated and the engine blew by me. My guardian angel saved me again. It was a great job as we got to sleep during the night on a wooden seat, which was uncomfortable. So sometimes I would sleep in my car. The tea we made by heating the water in the fireplace had a unique taste. We played cards with the shunters until our shift ended, so I felt guilty when I picked up my pay check.

But then I got drafted into the Army. I decided to enlist, so that I went into the Army itself instead of what is called the National Service. This was during the Vietnam War.

I volunteered for three years. I was in the infantry, and was supposed to have one year of special training for jungle fighting, then serve 18 months in Malaya and Singapore, and then six months in Vietnam. I thought my unit would be shipped overseas right after we finished basic training, but that kept getting postponed. They only wanted to have so many troops there at a time, and would wait for one battalion to be relieved before another battalion was shipped over.

I never did get overseas, never did see active duty. But there was plenty going on, nonetheless. Some of it was funny, some was boring, and some was tragic. For instance, one guy was just walking back to the base with two friends one night, and got hit by a car. He died right away. It turned out he wasn't old enough to enlist and had to have his parents' permission to join the Army. And he died that way; it was a shame.

Another fellow in my platoon just wanted out and did all sorts of antics to get a discharge. His name was Kevin Dawkins, and I had gone to school with him in Dunedin Kevin and I were never really close but our families knew each other. As a matter of fact, my brother Phillip had a crush on Kevin's sister Kathy at one time. After he finally got out of the army, Kevin became a lawyer and was one of the men who rewrote the constitution of Australia. So there was a happy ending to his story, after all. He now teaches at Otago University as a law professor.

The first car I owned, the Humber Hawk, I had with me in the army. I was the only one in the platoon who had a car so when we went into the City of Christchurch on our weekend break they all wanted to come with me if they had missed the bus. I often had ten big guys in my car and it wasn't long before I had to replace the shocks. Of course nobody helped with the cost - just to get a few bob out of them for gas money was a pain.

I remember one close call. Having been up since 5 a.m. to run and train all day I went into Christchurch in the evening. It was about an 18-mile drive from the army base, Camp Burnham, and there were lots of long stretches of road. You guessed it.... I fell asleep! All of a sudden I was facing a tree. I managed to turn the wheel in time to just miss hitting it.

At the army base one of our training sessions was conducted over an obstacle course. We had to complete the course fully laden with our gear and rifle. There was a wall that I always had trouble with. In the evening, after dinner, I would go by myself and try and conquer that wall. Eventually I got over it.

One of the funniest incidents happened when we were in training at the camp called "Little Malaya." We were on simulated manoeuvres, living outside and sleeping in two-man tents. In the middle of the night, the order came to pack up and move on. So everybody's trying to wake up, get up and pack up all their gear at the same time. And the zipper on my sleeping bag got stuck – with me in it. My buddy was trying to help me get loose, and we were muttering and cussing and sweating and trying to hurry. Unfortunately, our difficulties came to the attention of the sergeant and the lieutenant. All the other troops had there gear on. They just looked at us – everybody had kind of frozen – and finally the sergeant said, "Not you, again, George" and walked away without another word.

He might have been remembering another incident which had happened not too long before that. We were carrying full gear and going through this simulated jungle, when I tripped on a tree root. I fell, and went down really hard, rolling over and over down a hill. Well, I got up and started walking again. But after only a few steps, I passed out. When I came to, I thought I was back home. The sergeant was loosening my collar. I don't know just what I said or did, but he wasn't real happy with me after that.

Another time we were on the firing range firing at targets using live bullets firing at targets. We unloaded, disconnected the magazine, and then pressed the trigger. Everyone else's gun clicked except mine, as I did not realize there was a bullet in the chamber. Bang! It fired. There was dead silence the lieutenant and sergeant ran over to me. The lieutenant screamed at me "there could have been a dead body in front of you" I was so ashamed I could have crawled in a small hole.

We were in the jungle in the middle of the night when we stopped to camp. When nature called, I walked in the pitch black to get away from the tents, as we were not allowed to use flash lights. I awoke the next morning to discover I was only a few feet from a sheer drop over a cliff.

The next night we were assigned to keep guard as the other troops slept, simulating what we would do in a war. When my turn came I nodded off, to awake to the corporal booting me in the rear. I turned around to curse him out when I saw the Chaplin and the rest of the platoon looking at me. So I bit my tongue. I guess I deserved it.

The night before we were to leave the jungle we had gathered around the camp fire. A big guy was teasing a smaller guy, when all of a sudden the small guy picked up a rifle and hit the big guy with the butt end on the forehead, creating a gash. I grabbed him and pulled him away. The big guy was okay after medical treatment. The small guy was rushed out of there by the MPs and sent to a military prison. It was a pity as he was a friend of mine.

Another time, my unit was assigned to meet the new Governor General. We were getting ready to go to Wellington to greet the new Governor General (the Queen's representative to New Zealand). We were drilling on the parade ground, and the Senior Sergeant Major was shouting out the orders. Unfortunately, he was so far away from us that he could only see the first row of the unit. And guess who was in the first row?

The Vauxhall Velox I had when I lived in Dunedin.

It just so happens that this car was made in the same town as where my brother-in-law came from Luton, Bedfordshire, England. He married my sister Nora George and had four boys.

Also I was fixing the manifold to the exhaust pipe in my brother-in-law's (Mervyn Cottle) garage - fortunately I had my head down in the engine, when I placed the wrench down touching both terminals on the battery - all of a sudden there was an explosion like a grenade going off. The battery was literally in pieces. Mervyn yelled out 'wash your face in water,' he was not a happy camper.

My Chevy Hatchback
This car was towed to a garage after breaking down on the highway. I had it repaired at a garage but was overcharged. They refused to reduce my bill so I took them to a 'small claims court'. The garage was represented by a lawyer whereas I represented myself. The Judge ruled in my favor and ordered that the bill be cut in half.

*This Honda is the car I had to dig out of the snow - it was literally buried
- to pick up my sister-in-law, who was pregnant with her son Morgan,
and husband in the most memorable blizzard of 1978 that was so bad
the State came to a standstill for a week.*

*This is me with a beard with my nephew Zane.
He is the one that released the hand brake as it
took off. Notice how tiny this Sedan is – it's
barely above my 4-year-old nephew's head.*

This car was in numerous accidents that nearly cost me my life.

2005 Pontiac Sunfire I own currently

Right. Well, there were a bunch of guys behind me cracking wise remarks and making jokes, but the Sergeant Major can't see them – he only sees me.

I'm in the front row, smiling and trying not to laugh. He yelled out to me, "What is your name?"

"George, sir," I said.

"Well, George, stop laughing."

"Yes, sir," I said. And we started up the drill again. But these guys behind me started in again with their jokes and wise cracks, and again I'm trying not to laugh. But again the Sergeant Major sees me, and hollers out, "George! Come here!"

Then he turned and hollered, "Sergeant Brown, take this thing to the guard house, and don't feed him for a week."

So off I went to the guard house. The Sergeant Major came into the cell I was in yelled at me and left. That was Saturday morning. I don't know what happened but I was released that afternoon. The only lasting effect was that often when I was walking around the army ground, one or another of these same jokers would stick his head out of the window and yell, "Take that thing to the guard house, and don't feed him for a week!"

Once it was clear to me that I wasn't going to go overseas until much later, I just wanted to get out of the Army. At first, I went AWOL. But I went back to the base and gave myself up after a short time. I spent a couple of weeks in the brink, and then I started going after a medical discharge. It just so happened that as I was waiting for the discharge, I was assigned to the office of Senior Sergeant Major Swaltz, the same man who sent me to the Guardhouse. I was just a general cleaner-upper and "go-fer," but we became friends. He wanted to make me a corporal, and have me continue to work for him, but I said, "Sorry, sir, I'm getting out." I got the discharge after a while, and went back home to work on the railways again.

This time, though, I wasn't working on locomotives but at the workshops where the trains were repaired. They wouldn't have me back on the locomotives because of my medical discharge and because they were downsizing at the time. Steam trains were being phased out, and diesel trains were coming in. I met Jim Churchman again around this time.

Jim was working at Hillside Railways, doing a fitter and turner apprenticeship. I remember meeting him and some of his friends in the work shed. They were boiling their jeans. That was a fad then – boiling your jeans to make them lighter and bleached-out looking. You would throw your jeans into the steam water and bleach them a real pale blue by boiling them for a long time. You couldn't buy bleached jeans off the rack in New Zealand (for $100 a throw), the way you can now in the States.

This is the emblem I wore when I was in the infantry.

The Platoon I was in first. I am 3rd from the left in the back row near the barracks and parade ground. This was called the 7th Platoon. We had a rugby side and I was captain.

Well, anyway, I had run into Jim when I worked at the railways. Things didn't work out for me at the workshops. I left the railway job and bounced around in a lot of other jobs. Eventually I went back to school, to Otago Polytechnic, and got certified as a boiler worker.

After that I got a job at the Burnside Freezing Works. The name of this company doesn't really tell what it was; it was actually a slaughterhouse and meat packing and freezing company. My brothers worked inside the plant, where the animals were killed and processed. I worked in the maintenance section.

Jim Churchman also worked in the maintenance section but in a different part than I did. He actually told me later on that he had helped get me the job. I hadn't known at the time that he put a word in for me. Jim would help me in so many ways which I am grateful for.

Jim has an engineer's license, and one of his responsibilities was to monitor the Freon ammonia, an extremely responsible job. They had engineers just like Jim working around the clock, seven days a week, monitoring the Freon ammonia. If it got above a certain level, it could explode, and blow up the whole place.

I worked right next-door to Jim in the boiler room. This is where the coal is handled. There's a certain type of coal used, and it got dumped in a huge section of the boiler room and then taken by wheelbarrow-loads to the hopper. Once it was in the hopper, you just pushed a button to feed the coal into the fire. The fire boils the water, and makes the steam and hot water. You can imagine the amount of hot water used – for steam, for

I worked on this steam train when I worked the New Zealand Railways. As a loco assistant on Sunday nights we would throw logs of wood and oil rags to get them ready for the week It was dirty work but I did not mind.

the freezers, to clean the meat and carcasses, and to keep the plant clean. Hygiene was the number one concern there, and a lot of steam and hot water were needed to run a hygienic plant.

I worked for the New Zealand Electricity Department, too. From the sound of it, you would think that was a kind of stodgy, unexciting job. But no. I worked out in the field, where the power pylons were put up, and lines strung, and new territory covered. It was really quite adventurous. The photographs on the following pages show one of the places I went. The caption reads "Monawaii, Deep South," but that doesn't really give you the right idea. The Deep South is about as far south as you can go in New Zealand. As you can see, there are steep, sharp mountains and the area is heavily forested. Just to get to Batching Plant A, we had to drive on a makeshift road with sheer drops on both sides, and boulders in the middle of the road. Right at first, I didn't know whether we would make it to camp or not. It was a nightmare. Afterwards, of course, I got used to it and became almost blasé.

But I was never blasé when Les, the man in the top picture, drove me and some of his Maori friends into the nearest town, 20 miles away, to make telephone calls. Les was himself a Maori, and he had reconditioned an old (I mean, really old) Chevy. He didn't have a driver's license and drove like a maniac. He gave a terrifying ride, but when it was over we'd all kind of start laughing – it had been scary and fun at the same time.

Les and I worked together with some other guys, and it was our job to mix the cement that anchored the power pylons to the mountain. It took 12 cubic feet of cement to hold the pylons in place. We mixed the cement in what was called Batching Plant A. The gravel and sand was dumped in a hopper from a front-loader, the cement bags were trucked in from Invercargill, and the water came from a waterfall behind the camp.

The trickiest part was the water. There was a big hose immersed in the stream just upriver from the waterfall. There was a filter in the hose. Now, you know what happens to filters. They have to be cleaned regularly, or they clog up. And when you went to clean the filter, you had to be extremely careful, much more so than with ordinary filters. Because if you were careless, if you slipped or missed your step – you would go right into the fast-running stream and be washed over the waterfall. Not a good idea.

But it was an incredibly gorgeous place to be. We were so isolated – 20 miles from a telephone and no radio connection. The Deep South is largely unspoiled wilderness. One of the things that stand out in my memory is how beautiful the birds were, and that there were so many of them. There was one particular bird, a type of parrot called a Kea, which would swoop down on anything shiny. Beautiful or not, those birds quickly became a menace.

We had a terrific cook, and the quality of the food made up for a lot of other troubles. He was a Russian who once had been a professional chef. He said he had worked in five-star restaurants, and the food he prepared for us sure tasted like it. He had become ill with cirrhosis of the liver, which is probably how he wound up in the Deep South of New Zealand.

Another tunnel project I worked on was the Manapouri Hydro Electric Project which was southwest of Monowai in a god-forsaken place called Deep Cove. They were making a tunnel through a mountain. On the other side was West Arm, Lake Manapouri. Initially the American Utah Construction Company had the contract but ran out of funds so the New Zealand Government took over the project which is how I got a job there. We lived on a merchant ship that eventually would be scrapped for metal. There were two of us to a cabin (it was so isolated there was not one building in the area for miles). My cabin mate was an electrician and a very fit guy. He finished fourth in the New Zealand marathon so I would go for runs with him. He would run sideways up the hill while I would be running straight huffing away just to keep up with him. It was an extremely damp climate and we hardly ever saw the sun. To get to my job in the tunnel I had to go by train. The journey took about an hour and it was a noisy ride.

I was assigned to the center of the tunnel close to where they were ready to break through. We had this high pressure hose that would blow the loose gravel off the rocks. It took six of us to control this hose. Jokingly one guy let go which resulted in the rest of us being lifted off the ground by the hose. The cement carriages would follow and pour the cement to create a tunnel. One time I was pulling on the steel rope and it took off. It whipped the gloves right off my hand; luckily it did not take my hand. I also helped pour the cement. The water you stood in would go right up to your waist. They constantly pumped water out of there.

I was there about eight weeks when all of a sudden I got a pinched nerve in my neck. I was struggling to breathe so I went to see the doctor. He sedated me for 24 hours and when I woke up they decided to send me to the hospital which was 200 miles away in Invercargill.

This where the cement trucks back up to transport the mix to different sites at the same time it mixes the cement.

Batching Plant A, Monawaii, Deep South. I worked for the New Zealand Electricity Department.

These power poles – the foundation required 12 cubic feet of concrete.

We travelled by Land Rover and drove through the night over unpaved roads. We got a jet boat across Lake Manapouri and then drove for miles over farm land to get to the hospital. I woke up the next day after being sedated. I stayed in hospital for a week and then went home to Gresham Street in Tahuna, Dunedin.

Chapter Eight

Rugby, and How It Led to My Marriage

According to the Wall Street Journal the concept for the American game of football derives from rugby. Rugby is played non-stop for 40 minutes. The game is divided into two halves with a 10 minute intermission at halftime. What is commonly known as the "third half" takes place in the bar. During the third half the players drink, sing, celebrate or drown in their sorrows, according to the outcome of the game.

Rugby was not just a game I played as a boy in the neighborhood but was a sport I pursued as a young man – a pursuit which also led to me pursuing a young woman until I gained her hand in matrimony.

While I worked at the Burnside Freezing Works, they created a rugby side. It was quite a big deal, with competitions in New Zealand, and tours all over the world. My brother Michael was one of the star players. Originally I was not part of the squad Michael was on because I was in a separate department. But one of the squad members decided to pull out, probably because he couldn't afford the time and money it took. So I took his place.

At first we weren't really an official Rugby Club but were just part of the Burnside Freezing Works. To be official, we had to become affiliated with the New Zealand Rugby Union. So we did. Then we were eligible to go on tours and play in international competitions. In 1972, we had a chance to go on a world tour but had to raise the money ourselves to pay for the tour. We did all sorts of things to raise the money. One of the best ways was by holding raffles. We would go into the main hotels in Dunedin on Friday nights and raffle off chickens. We wound up raising about half the money we needed by raffling chickens; the rest of the money came out of our own pockets.

On the rugby tour to Europe we were in a town called Llanelli, an old coal mining town where rugby is extremely popular. I noticed the women folk were really into bingo and played it night and day. The All Blacks were scheduled to play the local team, the Scarlets, who had some famous rugby players of their own.

Our team went to watch the game, which was played in the middle of the week. Somehow I got separated from my team mates and the Scarlets were getting the better of the All Blacks. So there I was amongst hundreds of Welshmen so I started cheering for the Scarlets. Wouldn't you? It was the only game the All Blacks lost on tour. The whole town of Llanelli was so ecstatic that they ran out of beer. In fact, there is a song called "9 to 3" celebrating their win over the immortal All Blacks. To this day they have kept that "9 to 3" score on their scoreboard. In fact the same thing happened in 1963 but it was in my late brother-in-law's hometown of Newport, Wales. My brother Michael used to tell his friends it was his brother-in-law who drop-kicked the goal that beat the All Blacks. Years later I would get to meet the famous coach of that team – Fred "The Needle" Allen -- in Boston and had my photo taken with him. Unfortunately for Wales their national side has only beaten the All Blacks once. The other time they won was extremely controversial.

When we were on tour one of our opponents wanted us to perform the famous Haka that the All Blacks perform before an international rugby match. None of us knew the Maori words so my brother Michael came up with the brilliant idea of using the towns in New Zealand with Maori names for the script and just go through the motions. The audience was none the wiser.

The tour was wonderful. We went all over, places I never could have gone to in the ordinary course of events. We all had a real blast. We won a lot of games and lost some. And we were all young and full of enthusiasm – hell-raisers, you might say. As a matter of fact, a newspaper in one of the English towns where we played (and lost) reported, "Maybe these guys from New Zealand aren't the best rugby players in the world but, boy, they sure know how to drink!"

There are two things that stand out in my memory about our tour of the United States – and only two. One was Disneyland in California. And the other was getting robbed. The robbery came first.

We had just arrived in the States, exhausted from the long plane ride. We got through customs and went straight to our motel near the airport. Enroute we weren't paying much attention at all to our surroundings because we were so tired. We certainly didn't pay any attention to the two black guys who were following us.

We checked into the motel, and my roommate said he wanted to go right to sleep. I did too, even though I was (just a little) tempted to go out drinking with some of our team mates. My roommate and I went right to bed, and right to sleep, as soon as we got to our room.

1972. I am in the middle row second from left.
My brother, Michael, is in the front row second from left.
Taken at Christchurch Airport just before we flew from New Zealand.

I don't know how long we had been asleep when
we woke up, almost at the same time. Both of us had

heard a noise from the next room. So we pulled our trousers on, and went to look. About this time, one of the guys who had been out drinking got back. So the three of us went into the next room where we uncovered two guys taking our stuff. As soon as they got a look at us, one of the robbers pushed my roommate (a really big guy) out of the way, and he and his buddy took off.

I started to chase them, and was running after them outside when somebody stuck his head out of one of the motel windows and shouted, "He's got a gun!" At that point, I gave up the chase and ran as fast as I could back to my room. I heard their car take off as I returned – they had parked it next to the motel. They had taken my brother Michael's suede jacket. That may not seem like much by itself but I had a good watch and a bunch of travellers checks in the pocket of the jacket. That's what hurt! It was ironic that the jacket was taken because Michael had swiped it from an unscrupulous taxi driver in Paris.

After that, it took us awhile to get back to sleep.

It seems like there ought to be more memories there, but Disneyland and the robbery kind of crowded everything else out. I think some of the other guys had the same experience, too, because nobody seemed to remember much about the time we spent in the States.

We played in different parts of Scotland, Wales, and England. We didn't play any games in Ireland because of the outbreak of Mad Cow Disease. Because some of our guys were Irish, they chartered a plane to Ireland and visited places their families had come from.

Me with three team mates going up the
River Rhine in Germany.
Can you see the vineyards on the bank in the background?

We went over to France on the Hovercraft. What an experience -- the first and only time for me. Then to Switzerland and then on to Germany.

For some reason, being in Germany was one of the most impressive times for many of us. You have to remember that the first organized European settlements of New Zealand didn't occur until the mid-1800s. There were Maori tribes there, but nobody put up any permanent structures until after 1840. That means that you hardly ever saw *anything* – any building, or house, or man-made structure – that was more than a hundred years old. So for those of us who hadn't been to Europe before the sight of buildings, churches, cottages, bridges, barns and cathedrals built 400, 500 or 600 years before was *really* awesome!

We went to Cologne where everything except the churches had been bombed out during World War II. They had completely rebuilt the city, and it was totally modern and new. But it was kind of ghostly, too, because you would look at all the new stuff and remember why the city had to be rebuilt.

We went to Heidelberg, too. Heidelberg was unique. Apparently nothing had not been touched by the war so you could imagine what Germany had been like way, way back. They had maintained their old traditions and culture. I remember that they had their main meal early in the afternoon. And there were a lot of cuckoo clocks. There was a huge cuckoo clock in the middle of the town square that made an incredible amount of noise at high noon every day!

It may have been in Cologne that I saw a guy steal something. I don't remember what it was he stole, but we saw him running hell-bent down the street. And then right after him came the guy he had stolen from – running almost as fast, and carrying a big butcher knife. I was about to step in, but the others I was with told me to mind my own business and "just leave."

Another time in Germany we were about to go into a restaurant that had a bar in it. Apparently there were some of our guys in there drinking and showing off. They had just gotten their bill, and started hollering and shouting that they had been cheated by their waitress. The people who ran the restaurant just closed it down, and called the police who side with the locals, no matter what. There was a language problem too – none of them spoke German. We never did get to go in.

We pulled some kind of stupid stunts, ourselves.

Back in England, in an older hotel, I saw a mouse in the hallway. It appeared to be about half-dead, so I picked it up and put it in one of the other player's bed. He was out drinking, and didn't return until 3:30 or 4 a.m. When he went to get in bed, he pulled the covers back and saw this mouse. For a minute, he couldn't tell whether the mouse was really there, or he had just had too much to drink. When he decided that the mouse was real, he nearly hit the ceiling. The rest of us were laughing so hard our sides hurt.

Another time, we were in Durham in the northern part of England. (This reminded me of one of Roger Whittaker's famous songs, "I'm going to leave old Durham town.") Durham is a really old city, with cobbled streets and sidewalks. We were staying at the Royal Durham hotel where Mary Queen of Scots had stayed in 16th century. There was a large goldfish pond in the lobby. Well, one of our guys had been drinking too much that night and was really blasted. He was so drunk that he returned to the hotel and ate one of the goldfish. I think another teammate had dared him. Anyway, he did it, and everybody ooh'ed and aah'ed and laughed a lot and then went up to bed.

But in the morning, as we were going through the lobby on our way to breakfast, we saw the manager and the assistant manager standing by the goldfish pond. The manager was counting the goldfish, and the assistant manager was taking notes. We just barely got through the lobby before we totally cracked up.

After a game in Bristol, England, we went to the theme park which had an *outstanding* roller coaster. We rode it more than once; it was an extremely scary thrill.

At the end of the tour, we were at Kings Cross in the heart of London. This was the last place we were going to stay, so we were in a five-star hotel – kind of living it up before we went home. We had a lot of fun in London. We toured Madame Tussaud's wax museum, and we met a boxer at the hotel who had once fought Muhammad Ali. That was neat.

I was in the hotel lobby when an American girl and her friends came in. They were on a sight-seeing tour and had complained about being put in "a sleazy hotel." They were pretty upset and making quite a scene. So the tour manager arranged for them to stay in the same luxury hotel where we were.

And that's how I met Paula, the girl who became my wife. She was the American girl. I liked the way she handled herself, and I struck up a conversation with her. While talking we discovered a couple of "coincidences" involving Irish Catholics. Paula mentioned that she was from Massachusetts, John F. Kennedy's home state. And she said that he was the first Irish Catholic President of the United States. That prompted me to share that I had attended an Irish Catholic school and had dropped out when I was 16. Then it turns out that Kennedy was assassinated the same year I quit school, the first of other coincidences involving the Kennedy family.

Well, Paula and I got to know each other a little bit in London before she went back to the States, and I went back to Dunedin. But we wrote back and forth for more than a year. I was 26-years-old then and wanted to ask Paula to marry me. My mother had died by this time, and there was really nothing holding me to Dunedin. So I decided to move to America. I went to Canton, Mass., because that's where Paula was. And then, not too long afterwards, I asked her to marry me. She said yes, and we were married on October 28, 1973.

We were married at St. Gerard Majella Church, a Catholic church on Washington Street in Canton, Mass. Paula's father lived in Canton, and this was their family church. That year, the time changed at midnight on the day of our wedding because of Daylight Savings Time. That caused a small problem for my brother-in-law's sister, Maureen, and her husband who came from New York for the wedding. Maureen was originally from Wales, and her husband was from New York. They were the only people at my wedding whom I actually *knew.* None of my family or friends had come from New Zealand so everybody else at the wedding was Paula's family and friends. Even my best man, David Oliver, was Paula's cousin.

Well, anyway, I had invited Maureen and her husband and told them the date, time, and location of the church. They drove up from New York the night before the wedding, and went straight to their motel. In the morning they got up and went to St. Gerard's for the wedding. But they forgot to turn their clocks back that night for Daylight Savings Time and I had forgotten to remind them.

They got to the church too early, I guess. The bride and groom were standing at the altar already. Maureen didn't see anybody she recognized, but then she didn't expect to, since I was the only one she knew. So everything is terrific; it's a beautiful wedding, ladies are crying – the whole nine yards. Except when the bride and groom turn around to leave the church, Maureen discovers she and her husband have just sat through the wedding of a pair of total strangers!

Well, when the wedding party had left the church, she stormed outside and saw me standing with my best man, waiting for my turn to go in. She ran up to me and started hollering at me, "What the hell are you doing out here? You're supposed to be getting married!" She was quite emotional. All the rest of us thought it was really funny. Maureen was the only one who didn't see the humor in the situation. Even Paula thought it was a stitch. She and her husband had given us a beautiful gold-plated, gorgeous glass vase.

Well, when we finally got to *our* wedding, everything went smoothly. It was beautiful. There were about 80 people coming to the reception in the

Parish Hall. I went to the Parish Hall, and down into the basement to get changed, as planned. Only I didn't realize that the door to the room where I was changing had been locked from the outside. And after I had changed, I couldn't get out. I was locked in. I started pounding on the door but nobody heard. Then I started yelling. Finally, somebody heard and came to let me out. Just what we needed on our wedding day.

We honeymooned in near Lake Ossipee in New Hampshire, at a cottage belonging to a friend of Paula's father. Lake Ossipee is in the middle of the state near the Maine border. It's wooded, and the fall colors were beautiful. We were there two or three days when all of a sudden Paula gets this agonizing pain in her lower back, right at the base of her spine. She was really suffering, so we came home right away and got her into the hospital. It turns out that she had a cyst which had grown right on the bottom of her spine. She had to have surgery right away. Once the surgery was over she was fine again. So there was a happy ending to our honeymoon, after all.

And then we started into real life – real married life.

Our Wedding Day
28th October 1973

Paula's family at our wedding

Chapter Nine

A Family of My Own

Paula and I settled in Quincy, Mass., close to where her family lived. That was fine with me because they were really the only people I knew in the States, except for Maureen and her husband.

The transition from single life to married life was made pretty easy for me, I think, by the fact that I had been brought up not just a Roman Catholic, but a *Lebanese* Roman Catholic.

The Lebanese are Maronites – and proud of it. The Maronites were originally a fifth century Christian community that gathered around a hermit whose name was Maroun. Maroun himself was an ascetic, following the traditions of Anthony the Great, Pachomius, and the Desert Fathers. After his death, the Maronites began to be persecuted by the Christian fathers of Antioch. Some 350 Maronite monks were hunted down and killed. The Maronites fled to the mountains of Lebanon for refuge. Their community was recognized and given spiritual sanction early in the sixth century by the Pope. But the Lebanese never forgot how dearly won their beliefs and practices were, and remained fiercely devoted to their religion. If not switched at birth, I would have been raised a Presbyterian instead of being brought up as a fiercely devoted Lebanese Roman Catholic. That says a lot.

I think our married life also was smoother than most because I always really liked Paula's family. Yeah, Aldo and Carmela were some pair! They were Italian descent but Aldo's family was Napolitano, from Naples, and Carmela's family was Sicilian. Not that it really made much difference but you put them together and stirred them up – you had some volatile mix!

Paula's father, who is very handy, made Paula and her sister a doll house each. He did it with coffee stirrers for the floors, sandpaper for the roof (which I suggested and supplied). It was a tedious job but he did a great job.

One of the stories the family tells about Aldo symbolizes what the man meant to me. As a Flight Engineer during World War II, Sergeant Aldo Napolitano was on a mission over Panama, looking for a plane that had been lost to rescue any survivors. He suggested to the pilot that he go to the back of the plane to look for the missing plane (which definitely saved his life). Something went wrong with the controls of the airplane he was in, and it went down, crashing into a group of trees. He yelled to his comrades but nobody responded. He managed to get out of the wrecked plane only minutes before it exploded. His crew mates were not so lucky.

So there he was – in a Panamanian jungle, with only his rations, a knife, and a vague sense of what direction to go in trying to find a village. I don't remember exactly how long he was out there alone. He was bitten by a poisonous snake but cut around the wound with his knife and washed the poison out in the stream he was following. He also was stalked by a cougar for some time. Aldo used to joke about the cougar, saying that he must not have liked Italian food, since the wild cat never attacked.

He finally saw a young boy on the trail, and followed him into a small village. There were native drums beating all the while, and Aldo only later learned that they were signal drums – alerting the military that one of their men had been found. It wasn't very long before a group of soldiers arrived, with an extra horse, to take him back to the base. As they were leaving the village, another poisonous snake appeared, but it was shot by the captain of the unit, and they went on their way without any further trouble. They reached the base, and within a few hours, Aldo was on his way back to his unit.

Fast-forward fifty years. There is an organization in Hawaii that searches for planes which went down during the war. They actually found the plane that Aldo and his men were looking for. It was only two miles from where Aldo's plane went down. Most of the aircraft was still intact and they also found bones of some of the crew. Somehow, somebody in this organization had heard Aldo's story and got in touch with him. They sent him photographs, and the story of their discovery. Aldo was always greatly moved by this. He retired as a Lieutenant Colonel.

Paula's mother, Carmella, was a tremendous person. She was a believing Catholic but didn't attend church often. She was an extremely warm person with a great sense of humor and was a great cook. She was one of these people overcome a lot of adversity - her father had died when he was very young, and Carmella's mother was left with seven kids under 11 years of age. They all turned out to be great people, so the mother must have been an amazing woman. I think Paula inherited a lot of her grit from that side of her family.

When we were first married, we lived in south Quincy, in a section called Quincy Point. We moved into a brand new, small six-unit apartment building. We were right across the street from a Catholic church, and near the General Dynamics plant. I was back in that neighbourhood not too long ago and, of course, things have changed. Where General Dynamics was located there is now a big car dealer with all his automobiles displayed out in the yard.

We really liked that apartment. It was very comfortable, not too far from the city, and so situated that it was handy to every place we wanted to go. Paula fixed it up really nice. We started to settle in and meet people.

I have developed some really good friendships since moving to America. People like Derek and Lois Lugg. Derek, who also grew up in New Zealand, helped me get a job when I first arrived.

Derek and Lois Lugg

Other great friends I met at Montilios are Tim and Marela who are originally from Albania. They have two great kids. They have their own bakery now and are doing very well.

One of the guys I met at rugby practice was Kevin Hanley. He was Irish, and had refereed big rugby matches. While he was still in Ireland, he had met a girl from Quincy. They fell in love and got married. Kevin and I found some other guys interested in rugby, and before you knew it, we had a team. It was great fun, and something I had not expected to happen when I moved to the States. Rugby is more popular now than it was then. I have a photograph of President George W. Bush playing rugby at his college; he is about to tackle another player. Also, former President Bill Clinton played rugby in England while there as a Rhodes Scholar, and Ted Kennedy played rugby at Harvard. I never expected to be in such illustrious company, all because I had loved playing rugby all my life.

We lived in the apartment at Quincy Point for about three years. The problem was the rent. Not too long after we moved in, the rent began to go up. And up. And up. So in 1976 we decided to move out and go further south. We travelled down from Quincy to Pembroke, about 20 miles away. We found a small real estate office, a little building out in the middle of the boondocks. Years later the boondocks would be occupied by a mall and many other businesses, including a big car dealer, "Columbia" where I would buy the car I now drive.

When looking for a house, we first drove around to of get our bearings and we saw a lot of small spec houses for sale. Well, then we went to the real estate office. The salesman got out his books that showed the listings of houses for sale. I described one of the houses we had seen, and asked about it. He found a picture of it, but then said, "I don't know if you can afford it." And he keeps on turning pages. So I said, "No, let's go back to the one I'm talking about." The picture showed that it had been built on a hill, and that reminded me of Dunedin. So I said, "Let's go and take a look at this." He took us out to see the house, and I made an offer then and there – and we got the house, at the price I offered. Little did I know that my birth brother Jock and his wife Jan, who were living in Wisconsin before I moved to Pembroke, would actually drive past that town on the way to Cape Cod.

It was a real small house – a runt, really. We have since built on quite a bit. And it's where we still live. We have put a lot of work into that house, made a lot of improvements. We had a builder add a second story, and he did major remodelling inside. I did all the staining and painting.

We made a lot of changes in the yard, too, doing most of the work ourselves. When we were going to add the second floor, for instance, I took the wood from the old roof and made a tree house. I also made some playground stuff – swings, a see-saw, and tires piled on top of each other to play on.

I had to redo the leach field. That involved digging up practically the whole yard. Eventually we put down 4,000-square-feet of sod to finish it off.

I made a bocce court in the back yard. That was some job. I did it all by hand, using a wheelbarrow and a shovel. It took Adam and me about two months of hard labor to get it done. As it happened, I was out of work at the time, so I was glad to have something to show for that period of unemployment. The court is 70 feet long and eight feet wide. One end of it is a retaining wall, made from trees I had cut down around the yard. I got my photo with the bocce court in it, in a local paper. The headlines were "Fred's his name Bocce is his game."

I invented this to cut squares in a straight line for use in the bakery business.

*Paula in the vegetable garden of the house
we bought in 1977 (before the addition).*

*In February 1985 – we added on to our house.
Here are some photos of the work in progress.*

Jessie, Adam and Le-Ann (Jessie's friend) by the tree house. I have since pulled it down to make a green-house. The original 6'x2' came from the old roof of our house.

Our house after all the work was completed.

When the kids got too old to use the tree house, I pulled it down and used the wood to make a greenhouse. I used old storm windows for the sides and the roof. The 12-foot-square greenhouse is insulated, and contains a wood stove and cable TV along with some plants. You could practically live in it, if you wanted.

Adam, Lauren and Jessie – I am in the process of putting bricks down on the walkway.

Most recently, I made a brick pathway to the front door. I cut the path out by hand, and then traded for the bricks. I have a friend who had gotten the bricks for free. I wanted those bricks. And I had a lathe that my friend wanted. We did an even trade, and we both came out well.

I was pleasantly surprised at how easy it was to get adjusted to married life. I was 27-years-old, and Paula and I liked different things. I liked outdoor sports –

rugby, of course -- and I was big into running. Paula was an indoor girl. Also, I mainly read the newspaper, to keep up with world news and sports. Paula likes to read books. But the differences didn't seem to make trouble for us. There were lots of things we liked to do together.

Adam (2 ½) and Jessie (7) on the see-saw I made.

We both love movies, going to casinos, and travelling. And we were both pretty devout Catholics, too, so that made a difference in terms of stability right from the start.

Paula is very responsible and extremely good at handling money. She has worked as a bookkeeper most of her life, and worked at the State Street Bank in North Quincy until taking an early retirement a few years ago. That's a branch of a big bank in Boston that caters to institutional investors, so Paula had dealt with mutual funds a lot, and had a lot of experience with the stock market.

The responsibilities of marriage and family were not hard for Paula to handle because she was accustomed to taking care of things, always competent, and not inclined to shirk her obligations. She knows how to have a good time, and loves to have fun, but she's the serious one of the family.

One of the things I'm kind of proud of in my life is that I settled down and worked steady after we were married. Before that, in New Zealand, I bounced from job to job. I was a very reliable worker but was unsettled, without a career.

Jessica – aged 3 years and 10 months in her mother's boots.

Adam and bushwackers

Me in 1983

When I first came here, I worked at Boston Envelope, where (surprise!) they make envelopes. Then I worked at the Pneumatic Scale Company on Newport Avenue in Quincy. I worked in the maintenance department, and I really enjoyed it because I was always doing something different. I would be putting up shelves one day, and the next day would be adjusting some of the sophisticated machinery that made boxes or wax paper inserts. I was there for a couple of years. It just so happens there is a Stop & Shop supermarket there now. I currently work for Stop & Shop in Pembroke in the deli department, only four minutes from home.

Some of the things I used to do to supplement my income were to pick up air conditioners, sleep sofas, or any appliance that was left on the side of the road and sell them in the newspaper. The Patriot Ledger offered free classified ads for anything less than $50. I also would get up early in the morning in the summer time, drive down to Duxbury beach, and pick up cans and bottles at five cents each. I would come back with my Saturn wagon full of returnable worth up to $50 dollars, much like when I was a kid collecting lemonade bottles. More recently I delivered The Patriot Ledger (more than 160 on my route) in my car six days a week, also reminiscent of my younger days

Then I decided to become a hairdresser.

Yes, a hairdresser.

Paula's uncle operated a hairdressing school, called Debonaire Academy. It seemed like a good opportunity, so I took the course, passed the state board exam, and began working as a hairdresser. I enjoyed the work, mostly because I like meeting people and talking with them. It also seemed like a kind of quirky pay-out for all the times I "ran for my life" when my dad was going to cut my hair.

But after a couple of years, I decided to go into the bakery business. And it turns out that was really where I belonged.

When I used to help Mum around the house, I helped her make bread pudding. When I was older, I had worked at Godfrey's Bakery in Dunedin for awhile. But I never thought of baking as a career until I started working at Martin's Bakery in North Abbington, Mass. I didn't know it when I started but Martin's was actually one of the first commercial bakery ever established in the United States. They've been in business since the early 1800s. I only stayed at Martin's for a couple of years, and then went to work for Montilio's.

Montilio's is a famous bakery on Adams Street in Quincy. They are primarily cake-bakers, and are known all over. They do wedding cakes, birthday cakes, and cakes for almost any special occasion you can think of. They bake enormous cakes and cakes of peculiar shapes – cakes that look like buildings, or people. Some of the cakes were so large that they had to be put on big sheets of plywood for the base. Some of them couldn't be taken out of the building without moving the mixers etc.

Montilio's, which is more than 50 years old, had a fire there in October 2006. The two-alarm fire did a lot of damage. I hope they're able to reopen soon. They have baked cakes for everybody from Tip O'Neil to Queen Elizabeth.

Montilio's baked President Kennedy's wedding cake. Actually, there was a problem with that because Montilio's was working with non-Union labor. Somehow word got out, and it raised a stink because JFK was a pro-union Democrat. This caused a big controversy at the time which everybody has forgotten now, of course.

I was one of the bakers who made the cake for President Ronald Reagan's inauguration. We baked the cake in sections, put the icing in buckets and loaded the buckets and all the decorations (and all the decorators!) in a tractor-trailer truck and sent it to Washington DC.

They served the cake, but because it had not been vetted by all the security people, President Reagan never got to see it. He only saw pictures of it.

I was still working at Montilio's when they baked the cake for the Kennedy wedding at Martha's Vineyard in 1999. This is the one that didn't happen – the one that John Kennedy Jr. and his wife and sister-in-law were flying to when their plane crashed in the ocean.

This is me in Montilio's Bakery, Quincy, Mass.

I did a lot of moonlighting, too. I worked at Grahn's Bakery in West Quincy for five years. That's where I learned to make Swedish pastry. The day after

Mrs. Grahn died, the family closed the bakery. So I started making the Swedish pastry and distributing it myself to restaurants and clubs. I didn't have an electric mixer so mixed everything by hand in the basement of our house, which I had fixed up as a bakery kitchen. I used to bake all night, and deliver the pastry in the morning.

One time I had finished baking early and after loading everything into my Ford Ranger, I still had some time before all the pastry needed to be delivered. So I left the car parked in the driveway, locked the doors, and went in the house to take a nap. Well, the local squirrels got whiffs of the cardamom spice in the pastry, and did their darnedest to get into the Ford Ranger. They even chewed the rubber around the doors and windows. Fortunately, I woke up and came out before they really got into the car. Those were mighty hard-working and mighty disappointed squirrels!

At this point in my life I believed I was of Norwegian descent on Mum's side. Later, through research by my younger brother Phillip George, I learned Mum really was Swedish, not Norwegian. Either Mum was unaware of her Swedish background or was misinformed. Phillip discovered Mum's grandfather was a Pearson (Persson in Sweden). Had I known the truth I could have told Mrs. Grahan I was Swedish and maybe she would have left me the bakery in her will. Later in my life I became a member of the Viking Club believing I was Norwegian, only to find out I was not Norwegian but Swedish. But at least I was

Scandavian until, that is, I learned was switched at birth and was really neither. Confusing, huh?

While I was moonlighting, I did a lot of different jobs. I got into landscaping, mowing lawns and pruning trees. I have worked for Mike and Susan Wolf for more than 20 years.

Mike and Susan Wolf's winter home in Nasara, Costa Rica

They're a real nice couple who live in Marshfield and have a beautiful winter home in Costa Rica. But their Marshfield house has a spectacular view of the North River, so I always feel rejuvenated after I've worked on their lawns and trees.

I worked for a Haitian bakery for a couple of years. I was the only Caucasian working and introduced different patties that became an instant success. They made pre-cooked patties of spicy meat, chicken, and fish. I introduced some with sausages and onions, bacon and eggs, and some cheese spreads.

I also worked for Valle's restaurant where I introduced their now-famous peach shortcake. They went out of business. Nothing to do with my peach-shortcake, I hope!

I also worked making bagels for a Jewish bakery in Canton and for a Jewish caterer. I remember an awful mishap with the caterers. I was breaking dozens of eggs into a bucket, and one of the eggs had specks of blood in it. Ordinarily, that happens and doesn't really matter. But these were kosher bakers, and I had to throw out the whole bucket of eggs. Fortunately, that had never happened to me before and it sure never happened again!

After a hiatus I was back working at Montilio's – four years at the original bakery, run by Ernie Montilio, and then ten years for George Montilio, Ernie's son. I worked for George right up through 2000. He had branched out from doing strictly baked goods and added such items as snacks, sandwiches, and quiches. And he delivered to restaurants, clubs, and supermarkets.

I really liked working for George Montilio. The cakes were a real challenge. Some of the cakes we made were humungous – like wedding cakes 24 feet in diameter. Now, *that's* a wedding cake! But I really liked almost all the work. Cookies, pastries, biscotti, strawberry shortcake, special Italian pastries – I did it all, and had a great time at it.

Along the way, quite a bit had happened. I ran the Boston Marathon in 1978. A friend put an entry form in for me and helped get me in. He was a Presbyterian minister from Northern Ireland – how ironic is that! Years ago there was a vocal Presbyterian Minister called Ian Paisley who was from Northern Ireland. He was very outspoken in politics and religion. He came across as anti-Catholic. Now I find out I have relatives who are Presbyterian ministers! I wasn't really qualified but I promised I would train like a dog. And I did. I ran 70 to 80 miles a week. I got as fit as a buck rabbit, and ran the marathon in three hours. I was quite proud of myself. The photo taken above was in the Quincy Marathon. I also ran in the Newport and Rhode

Island marathons. In all three you had to run the same course twice to complete 26 miles.

1978, the year of the Boston Marathon, also was the year of the big blizzard in Massachusetts. I don't know how much snow fell but practically the whole state was paralysed for a week. That also was the year that my sister-in-law (on Paula's side) was pregnant. She and her husband lived right on the ocean, and had to be evacuated to a public school nearby. Because she was pregnant, they didn't want to stay at the school, so they called Paula. So we went out there and picked them up at about 2 a.m. which happened to be, thank goodness we didn't know it at the time, the height of the storm.

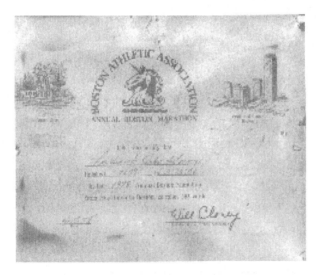

That was an unbelievable trip! I had just bought a little white Honda Civic. And here we are in the middle of a blizzard. I would drive for a ways, and then have to get out and clear the car off. But the white car and the snow blended together. And here I am, shovelling snow off the car which half the time I couldn't even *see!* It seemed to take forever, but we finally made it home. The next day my brother-in-law and I, driving in his four-wheel-drive vehicle, went back to their house. We stayed behind the building but we could see the waves coming in, hitting the seawall, and going right over. We saw part of the pavement floating down the road, and other cars.

So, what with the blizzard and the Marathon, 1978 was a banner year.

I later ran the Newport Marathon, and I ran the Quincy Marathon twice. All of these are 26-mile and 385-yard courses. It was a big deal for me to do this because I had been in plaster casts as a kid and was only four-years-old when I began to walk after the casts were taken off.

Paula and I had started a family. Our daughter, Jessica Ann, was born May 24, 1979. Paula had some trouble with that pregnancy, and the baby was delivered via caesarean section. I was in the room for the birth but they had a screen up about halfway down Paula's chest so I couldn't see the surgery. But I heard Jessie's first cry. And I saw her just minutes after she was born. It was one of the most moving experiences of my life.

Well, when the doctor was sewing Paula back up, she apparently contacted an infection. Within a few hours Paula was really sick with a raging staph infection. She was in the emergency room all night. and was delirious; she didn't know who I was, and didn't know who *she* was. It was like she was drunk. If it hadn't been life-threatening , it would have been funny.

(Here's another of those weird coincidences. Years later I cut my hand with a power saw, and needed stitches. I went to the hospital emergency room, and guess who stitched me up? The same doctor who delivered Jessie. I started to remind him of the situation with Paula, but he just ignored me. I'm sure he was embarrassed, and it later occurred to me that he might have been nervous about a malpractice lawsuit. All the same, it was weird to run into him again under those circumstances.

And here's one more weird coincidence, about my sister-in-law, Diane, and her son Morgan. I had left Dunedin for a flight to Wellington to get my visa to return to the I.D. For some reason, I placed the largest bet I had ever placed on a colt named Captain Morgan. The horse won, but before it did I was sweating bullets because I needed that money for my trip to the U.S. My nephew Morgan is now in the Air Force and his rank is captain – Captain Morgan!)

Me with Jessica and Adam

I absolutely flipped over Jessie. I was like a new dad out of a television sitcom. While she and Paula were still in the hospital, I went to visit them. On my way to the hospital, I passed a house where there was a lawn sale going on. And there, right in front, was a child-size play-table and little chairs. I bought them all right then, even though I knew it would be two or three years before she'd be big enough to use them. And I took them to the hospital with me to show them to Jessie.

Our son, Adam Christopher, was born March 14, 1984. No complications there, thank God. Both children were good from the start, and pretty easy babies. Jessie developed milk intolerance but her doctor told us to take her off milk and as soon as we did she was okay.

I missed a lot of things that happened with them when they were little because of the hours I was working on my regular job and because I was moonlighting. I worked long hours – 18 to 20 hours a day. I would finish at Montilio's, go out to my truck, take a nap for a couple of hours, and then go to whatever other job I was working. In the bakery business, especially around holidays, you work round the clock. I remember once on my birthday I worked 30 hours straight. The discipline and training and scheduling was mostly left up to Paula. I didn't have much time left to be around the kids.

But I enjoyed being a father. When they got older, and I wasn't working such crazy hours, I used to take them to the park. We had a good time. Also, I remember when Jessie was first starting to play soccer. I don't know how old she was but she seemed pretty little to me. We went to one of her soccer matches, and she was so excited she was literally jumping up and down before the game started. Then she was so excited that when the ball came to her, she ran the other way. We always have a big laugh when we tell that story which is still quite a bit too often for Jessie's liking.

We didn't have a lot of trouble with the kids. But no matter how good they are as a rule, you can't avoid having *some* trouble.

Vegemite is a strong vegetable extract spread you put on bread that we ate in New Zealand. It is great on fresh baked bread with butter and lettuce. It can also be used as a way of punishing kids if they swore. I would chase Jessie around the yard into the woods, if she swore, to put it onto her tongue as she hated it (that is how we got punished as kids when we were growing up).

Adam was a really good kid, but there was one time when he was 10- or 11-years-old that we had to call the police. I was missing some money. I don't remember exactly how much it was – not enough to break the bank, but a significant amount. Adam swore up and down that he didn't know anything about it. That's when we called the police. One of the policemen talked with Adam alone, and Adam broke down. An older kid who lived across the street from us had instigated the theft. He had influenced Adam and he wound up with the money. All in all, it wasn't a bad experience. We could see that Adam knew he had done a wrong thing and genuinely regretted it. We felt the whole thing was almost worth his learning that lesson.

Jessie was a follower, too. She would never start any trouble; she wasn't a real defiant kid or anything like that. But there were certain kids we didn't want her to hang out with. We could control it when she was home, but once she got to school there was nothing we could do. Jessie knew this, and took advantage of it. There were two girls, in particular, that I didn't want Jessie to have anything to do with. Like I said, she was a follower, and I was afraid these other girls would influence her in a bad way. Mostly it was okay, but every now and again Jessie would get rebellious and go along with them. A couple of times she had trouble in school, and had to talk with the principal.

Adam, me and Jess – 167 Elm Street

It's hard, though. When I was a kid we had certain rules and routines around the house. Somebody washed the dishes, somebody else dried, somebody else put them away. With rules you knew where you should be at certain times. And you had a certain time you had to be in bed. But it was hard for Paula and me to structure things like this for our kids, especially since I was working crazy hours. I know they are probably tired of hearing this but my children had it easier than I did growing up. We had to work harder – no dishwasher, no refrigerator, no washing machine or dryer. It makes a difference.

Adam, when he was in his early teens, ran into one of the kinds of coincidences I have seen so many times in my life. In school, Adam became friends with a boy named Phillip, who lived across town. Adam was talking with this kid's mother one day, and it turns out that she had come to Pembroke from Halifax, Nova Scotia. She was a person who was quite interested in genealogy and family trees. Then, as they talked further, it emerged that she had a distant relation who had not only lived in New Zealand but had run a business in Dunedin. Then it turns out the woman's husband came from the same town as Paula, grew up with her, and went to school with her for several years. Adam and Phillip, who are still friends by the way, got a real kick out of that.

My family life has really been extremely good. I have two very well-behaved children, and an extremely good and responsible wife. My in-laws have always been very supportive of me, and quite good to me.

Sometime in my mid-to-late 40s, though, I started thinking about my life: Whether I had done the right things; Whether I had made the right decisions at times; Whether my life was going the way it was intended. It doesn't sound like much, but here I was – my life was great, and yet I was still wondering.

Around this time, and over the next few years, I had a number of accidents – most of them near-fatal accidents, a number of them automobile accidents, some of them involving other people.

One memorable example occurred while I was going to work during a major snow storm with swirling winds. I drove my car to the driveway of the store but the driveway was blocked by a mound of snow. I decided to park my car at the top of this steep hill and walk down to the store. I put on my gumboots, took a cell phone, my work clothes, and started walking downhill. Halfway down the snow was practically up to my waist and I had to decide whether to continue downhill or return to my car. Fortunately I chose to return. I turned around, reached for a mound of ice created by a previous storm, climbed out of the rut I was stuck in, and retraced my steps to the top of the hill. I got into my car and drove another route to work, which took me a half hour to travel 200 yards!

Every time one of these accidents or near tragic events happened, I wondered what the point was. I have come to think that there was a work – a kind of personal work – that I needed to do before I died. I certainly believe that now, in light of the switch. If I had died in any of those accidents, there's a lot I would not have known, and a lot I would not have been able to do. At the time, I didn't think in terms of "God spared me" but now I do.

Adam, me and Jess

During the 1975 oil embargo gasoline was being rationed and this caused long lines at the gas stations. One day I went to this particular gas station for the first time. I overheard the attendant, Paul Mills, talking to someone about how his grandfather had come to the USA from England. He had "jumped ship" but because he had created a business (a butcher shop) in upstate New York he had been allowed to stay. One thing led to another and it turned out that his brother, George Mills (Paul's great uncle) had started a butcher shop just down the road from where we lived in Forbury Road and it is still there today. There was a tribute to George Mills in the newspaper in Dunedin as he was still working there at the grand old age of 100!

One time I was playing a game of cricket. The opposition was batting and I was fielding when the batsman hit the ball past me. One of my team mates picked the ball up. He was a big guy and he threw it really hard. The batsman ran towards the other end. I ducked as I was in line with the wicket and the cricket ball (which is probably the hardest ball in any sport) hit me square on my ear. Everything went black. I literally saw stars. Michael ran over and grabbed the guy but it was only an accident. Had it been a little lower it could have been fatal.

I think this string of things started maybe around the early '90s. I was driving a Ford Ranger at the time, and in the winter had very close accidents on snowy roads where the brakes locked. Once, I couldn't stop at an intersection and just flew across it. No cars were coming, so there wasn't a collision, but my heart was in my throat. The second time, the car went into a skid and was out of control. I wound up doing a 180-degree turn, slamming onto the bank on the other side of the road. Again, no cars were coming. The third time, I was still lucky in that there wasn't a collision. But I was driving in heavy traffic and went into a skid. The car spun across the road, and I found myself facing the opposite direction, sandwiched between two cars.

There were other accidents, too.

I was changing the oil on the Ford Ranger, and had it up on a new hydraulic jack. I didn't have any business trying to do that job at that time because I was half asleep after working all night. But I thought I could get it done. I had forgotten to put wedges behind the tires, so when I let the jack down, the car suddenly started to roll down our steep driveway. I tried to get into the car as it was rolling but couldn't. The car rolled right across the street (no kids around or on-coming cars, thank God!), and headed down an embankment and into my neighbor John O'Neil's yard. I remember seeing that John had just come out of his work shed, with a trowel in his hand. Well, the Ford Ranger hit the shed and totally knocked it off its foundation. The tow truck hauled the Ford Ranger out and then had to haul the shed back, damaging the driveway considerably. At least John got a new driveway.

Once, my father-in-law had brought his car over to our place, and asked me to push it since he was having trouble with transmission. He was in the car with his wife Carmella when I came out of the house. I lifted the back of the car and it must have jumped into reverse because it took off. The next thing I knew – the car was out in the middle of the street (having barreled down our steep driveway), and Carmella was yelling at Aldo, "You could have killed him!" I realized that, as I went up to the car, I thought to keep my feet away from the wheels. I not usually that cautious but if I hadn't been I might have been killed.

Another time, I was helping Aldo trim some branches off a tree in his yard. I was up in the tree, using a chain saw, and it slipped (still running) out of my hand as Aldo was walking under the tree. It missed him by no more than an inch or two.

I was coming home from work late one night, and inadvertently drove the wrong way down a one-way street. Another driver, coming fast, broadsided me, and spun my car completely around. Fortunately, it was an open area so neither of us really got a direct impact. Neither one of us was hurt.

Another time, I had dozed off while I was driving. I woke up hearing a voice – my guardian angel's voice – saying, "Watch! Wake up!" I woke up and slammed on my brakes almost at the same time. Even so, I ploughed into the car in front of me. The front end of my car was smashed ($6,000 worth), but no one was hurt badly.

In the same car (Saturn SW1) I was driving to work one day when the car was only six months old. I was wearing my seat belt, and that probably saved my life. Traffic was fairly heavy, and the cars in front of me were slowing to a stop. I had my brakes on and was slowing down, too, when I looked in my rear view mirror, and saw a bread truck coming right toward me at a high speed – and definitely not slowing down. The driver had dozed off (his guardian angel apparently failed to wake him up, or maybe they weren't on speaking terms that day!), and he just kind of *exploded* into my car with such force that it pushed my car – at a dead stop, and with the brakes on – into the rear of the car in front of me. His truck hit me so hard that, if I had not been wearing my seat belt, I would have gone through the windshield. As it was, I rammed into the steering wheel and was then thrown backwards with enough force to break the seat. I had a three-seated car until the seat could be replaced. I was unconscious briefly, and woke looking up at the ceiling of the car. Ambulances and policemen were all around, but I wasn't hurt, so I made my statement, and went off to work.

I still remember the date of one of the worst of the accidents: August 8, 1996. I had been fixing my daughter friend's bicycle at home. I finished up around five o'clock. I rode the bicycle partway around the block, and turned down a steep grade around a blind corner and looked straight into the front of a Ford Windstar which was coming at me at about 50 mph. It was one of those times where you don't see things happen consecutively – it's all jerky, like looking at slides or frames, not a smooth film. I saw the SUV coming toward me. I froze, and got hit square on. I could see myself literally flying over the hood. I do not remember hitting the windshield. Then I must have lost consciousness for a minute, but I remember hearing a woman screaming. The next thing I remember is being fully conscious. I was on my back, looking up at two big policemen who didn't know – or didn't care – that I was conscious.

"I think he has a serious head wound," one of them said. I didn't know at the time what an understatement that was!

Apparently I was taken by ambulance to Route 3, where traffic was stopped and I was put in a helicopter and airlifted to Boston Medical Hospital. I was in surgery for four hours, and had 70 stitches in my face. Beyond that, I had a bruised kidney that kept me in a lot of pain for a while, but I was only laid up for two weeks before I went back to work. I still have the front wheel of the bicycle I was on; it is bent out of shape.

This is the front wheel of the bicycle I was on after I was hit head-on by a Ford Windstar SUV.

I also have had a couple of accidents happen where I should have been seriously injured, and yet I walked away with only some bruising. I built a horseshoe course in our yard one year. The following spring, as I was mowing the lawn for the first time in the season, I tripped over the wooden border around the horseshoe course. I fell full force onto the steel rod (the one you throw the horseshoes at). I landed on the rod on the fleshy part of my side, just below my ribs. The force of my fall drove the rod into the ground six inches. I was wearing a shirt and a windbreaker. I got an indentation in my side, but the rod did not even break the skin. I was winded for a while, and had a good-looking bruise, but that was all.

A few days after that fall, I fell again. I was trimming bushes around the cellar bulkhead in the back yard when I slipped. I had the clippers in my hands, so I could not break my fall. I came crashing down, half on and half off the bulkhead. Again, I was winded and had significant bruising, but my ribs were not broken, and there were not even any cuts.

Afterwards, after I learned about the switch, I looked back on all the accidents, all the doubts, all the questions I had about where I had been and where I was going, and thought maybe all this was like a premonition.

I didn't know anything about this other family, or this other history, at that time. But somehow the possibility, or the thought, that everything might somehow have been different really had started bugging me. And actually, I think it was my family that helped me through that time. Not by anything that they *did*, exactly, because I don't think they even knew what was going on with me at the time.

Me with Paula's father, Aldo Napolitano – aged 92 at his Commemoration in November 2006

But it occurred to me that, if everything had been different, there would have been no Paula, no Jessie, no Adam, and no strong, great relationship with Paula's folks. None of that would have happened.

And I realized that I wouldn't have wanted to do without any of that – not for anything. And I got a measure of peace, and a sense that there were things in my life as it was that were irreplaceable, and more precious to me than I had known or could ever hope to say.

We have had a timeshare in Cape Cod for many years. Sometimes we go there in the summer months or we give our week up to a relative. We have at times "exchanged" it for one in some other part of the world.

We also have a place in Mauri, one of the Hawaiian Islands. We have been there three times. It is a beautiful island. Our place is right on the ocean with volleyball net, a swimming pool and a lovely beach. There is a trip on the island called the "Road to Hana". It is a scary trip with narrow roads and sheer drops into the ocean with magnificent views. It is where Charles Lindenburgh lived and he is buried right on the edge of a cliff. Also Oprah and Jim Nabors have land there.

We went across to see the Island of Molokai where Father Damien was famous for living amongst and caring for the lepers. There is a church and a statue of him where he is buried. It is also famous for Macadamia nuts which require little maintenance as the trees (roots above the ground) do not require water and the nuts grow at different times on the same tree. Like the Cape Cod timeshare we have it for one week a year.

Paula and I took the kids to New Zealand. Jessie was nine years old, and Adam was about five. We had a terrific time. We also took the kids to Disney World in Florida, and to the Bahamas where they went on a banana boat. The banana boat is not the kind Harry Belafonte sang about but is a large inflated, bright-yellow banana, with handles for people to hold on with. The banana is pulled by a boat, while all the riders bounce up and down on the banana to give themselves a more exciting ride. Everybody has life jackets, and the boat driver makes sharp turns which sometimes cause the banana to spill over. It's kind of like a carnival ride, except you're in the ocean. And I did something I had wanted to do for a long time – I went parasailing. This is where you get harnessed to a parachute, and tied to a boat which "launches" you up into the sky. The boat moves along and keeps you floating in the air, and you see everything from the sky -- the whole island with the sandy beach looking pearly white and the sea like turquoise. It was even better than I had hoped.

Then there was the time that Paula and I took a land-sea cruise. That was really fantastic. We flew from Boston to Salt Lake City. We toured the city, saw the museum which showed how Salt Lake City became what it is today, and went to the Mormon Tabernacle. The Tabernacle isn't as large or as old as the cathedrals I had seen in Europe but it promoted the same feelings of awe. Amazing.

We took a bus from Salt Lake City to Little Falls, Idaho, and then to Butte, Montana. Because of the vast copper deposits in the hills, Butte had been a notorious mining town in its heyday between the last of the 19th century and about 1920. They said that a third of all the copper produced in the U.S. at that time came from Butte, and that the city attracted workers from Ireland, Wales, England, Finland, Serbia, China, Croatia, Montenegro, and Mexico. There's lots of history there, and lots to learn that you wouldn't otherwise know. We were fascinated by what was once the longest-running house of prostitution in the States – the Dumas Brothel. This has now been turned into a museum, and a tribute to the rough old days when Butte was a boom town.

From Butte, we went to Yellowstone Park to watch Old Faithful blow its top right on schedule, and then on to Wyoming and South Dakota. The route we took is just bursting with history – the gold rush, the silver mines, Custer and the Indians, Wyatt Earp, Wild Bill Hickok. We saw Calamity Jane's tombstone at Boot Hill Cemetery. It was called Boot Hill because they buried the outlaws there with their boots on. We drove through the northernmost part of Idaho, and saw the most beautiful country you could imagine. Then we went through the Grand Tetons to the Grand Coulee Dam across the Columbia River, then to Spokane, Washington and up to Vancouver and then took a cruise boat up into the southeast passage of Alaska.

The Alaska part of the trip was incredible. The cruise ship docked in Juneau, where we took a helicopter ride and landed on the Great Mendenhall Glacier. No matter what pictures or movies you have seen, nothing prepares you for the actual *experience* of the glacier. You look down a crevice, it seems like for miles, and yet the ice is sparkling white, and there is the bluest, most brilliant water running underneath. We took a sea plane ride and landed on the water near Skagway, Alaska. This was a mining town with mountains going straight up on three sides, and water on the fourth. Miners in the Gold Rush days sailed to Skagway and then took a train to the Yukon. So we rode the narrow-gauge railway up through the rugged mountains and into the Yukon Territory, and on to the Yukon River. Then back to Liarsville, on the outskirts of Skagway, where we saw the Gold Rush Museum and the old miners' camps. What a rough and lonely life that must have been! A lot of people were misinformed by the media in Seattle so hence the name "Liarsville." The ones that made it rich were the merchants.

We ended the trip in Seattle where we took a great tour of the city before flying back to Boston. All in two weeks!

We have done other travelling through the years – sometimes with the kids, and sometimes just the two of us. We went to Las Vegas a couple of times, and to Hawaii. And I took Adam to Europe once. And we all went to New Zealand together.

Some years before this, my brother Peter and wife Lesley had adopted a little boy named William. They also adopted a girl named Jessie. And then they had their own son, Ben. Well, when I took my family to New Zealand, William had a terrible accident.

Peter had bought a house at Port Chalmers. Peter and Lesley did wonders with it as it was a shack when they first brought it and they sold it for a big profit. Peter's house is right on the edge of a cliff on the coast near Dunedin. It's a very hilly spot, and is rocky all the way down to the ocean.

Well, William and brother Ben had rigged up some ropes that they would swing on, in the trees on the edge of the property. They did this a lot, and it didn't seem like anything particularly dangerous to them.

On this particular day, William was swinging as usual. But something happened – either the rope broke, or his hand slipped -- and he fell down the rocks and smashed his head open.

Ben was with him, and ran to get their mother. William was taken to the hospital in an ambulance, and had major surgery that night. Peter and Lesley stayed with him all night, and had the other children stay with friends.

Paula and I had taken our children to Central Otago for the day, and when we got back to Peter's house, nobody was home and we couldn't get in the house. So we stayed the night at a motel. We didn't find out until the next morning that William was in the hospital. He had to have surgery once or twice more after that. And he had to learn how to walk and talk all over again. But now he's fine. He was a mechanical genius before this accident, and he's still a computer whiz today.

They have homeless shelters in Boston - one for women called Rosie's Place and across the road is a place called Pine Street Inn for men. In Quincy they have a place called Father Bill's for anyone. Years ago when I worked at the bakeries I used to take the bread or pastries that did not sell to the shelters the next day. I remember taking some to Father Bill's place. I ran into him on the way out after making a delivery. I told him that I had just made a delivery but he most likely did not hear me and he said to me "Did you enjoy your stay here?" "Sure Father" I said and went on my merry way.

William, Jessie and Ben

I got my GED about the same time as my daughter got her's in Quincy as I did not graduate in New Zealand as I had quit school early.

Jessie got interested in nutrition as she got older. She worked in the health food business for quite a while. She is actually a vegetarian now, which has caused a little friction between her and her partner. He is not a vegetarian, and is not interested in becoming one, and he's a great cook to boot.

Jessie's husband is from the island of Dominica in the West Indies. He is a cricket fan and a good player. It helps both of us that I know quite a bit about cricket; it gives us something in common, and it rescues him from only being able to talk with people who don't know a cricket bat from a baseball bat.

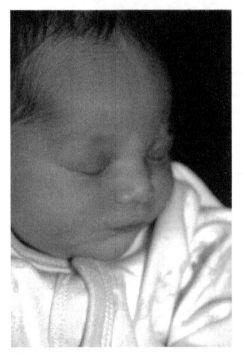

We are proud grandparents now. Jessie gave birth to Samuel Marley Jean-Baptiste on March 2, 2007 at 7:24 p.m. which happens to be March 3 in New Zealand (as it is 18 hours ahead of America).

Therefore my grandson, Samuel Marley, shares the same birth date as his great-grandparents - Helen Churchman and her late husband, Gordon (my birth parents). Mrs. Churchman is one year older than her husband. All the grandchildren refer her as Mama.

Jessie is now working as a nurse's aide. She likes it a lot. She's good with people.

Adam went to Green Mountain College in Vermont. He's interest in environmental issues but quit school after three years. He went to Italy and then to New Zealand. Actually, he loves New Zealand. He became a citizen, and will probably move there sometime soon. He may complete his college education there. I hope so. Adam has learned about the uniqueness of New Zealand, including that it is the first country to introduce Social Security and the first country to allow women to vote. (An American woman travelled to New Zealand and pushed suffrage through Parliament.)

Fred, Fran and Jason Everson taken at the Cedar Club

Back in 1970 when Mum became quite ill with severe chest pains Fran made the right decision to take her to her house where she would die that night. The last thing she said to me was "I will be alright, Fred." It was extremely hard on Paulette and the younger ones to see her suffer. My brother Paul took it extremely hard. He broke down uncontrollably when he came home from sea to attend the funeral. He blamed the doctor but that was not his fault.

Jim Churchman was amongst the many people who would attend my mother's funeral but, in reality, it was Jim's birth mother's funeral. The next day my George cousin's husband Paddy was telling his workmates at coffee break what a great woman Mrs. George was. After making that observation Paddy was about to get into his brewery tanker to drive off when he died. He was buried the day after next to my mother's grave.

I was living in the United States when our father died in 1980. I took it extremely hard but was not able to attend his funeral.

My nephew, Jason, is the son of my sister Fran and John Everson from Newport, Wales. Jason was living in London when the 1999 Rugby World Cup was being played. I decided to take Adam, then age 15, over there with me. I had arranged to stay in a time-sharing place in Normandy, France for a week and the other week at Jason's apartment in London.

We got to see all the historic sites in London. We went down the River Thames, saw Big Ben and the Tower of London, we took a double-decker bus around the city and saw St Paul's Cathedral where Prince Charles and Lady Diana Spencer were married. Incidentally that is where the concept of the original wedding cake came from. A chef was trying to think of something different for his daughter's wedding when he noticed the shape of the cathedral was three tiered so that is where the wedding cake concept, which most bakers abide by today, originated. We got to see

Piccadilly Circus, the famous London Bridge (the original bridge was bought by a wealthy American, dismantled and rebuilt in Arizona).

Adam and I took a train from London to Portsmouth to catch the ferry to France. When we arrived it was Sunday morning and the ferry was not due to leave until that night. So, we looked around and found a nice restaurant to eat in. The evening came and we got on the ferry. By this time we were hungry again and as everyone seemed to speak French we found it hard to communicate. I asked the chef for something to eat and he looked at me and said "You lorry (truck) driver?" I said "Okay" and he got Adam and me two French bread rolls with ham, tomato and lettuce - no condiments. We did not care as we were so hungry. The sleeping beds were all lazy boys.

We arrived in this historic city of Cannes and were greeted by statues of Joan of Arc and billboards advertising the movie "Joan of Arc." Maybe it was her home town.

We got a bus into the city centre and I noticed a lot of school children getting on the bus. As they walked by their classmates they would kiss each other on the cheek as a way of greeting. I thought it was such an unusual custom.

We got into the city and there was a huge cathedral that was more than 600 years old. Again we could not communicate with the people so we had to walk with all our suitcases as nobody knew what "taxi" meant. We must have walked about ten blocks when we discovered that all their transportation was centralized i.e. Trains, taxis, rental cars, buses. So I purchased a ticket to go to our place in Annabella at 4 p.m. It was noon so I sat down and fell asleep to wake an hour later to discover that Adam had gone sightseeing without telling me. I was sweating "bullets." Again I had a problem with the language as I tried to explain to the police ... they just shook their heads. With about ten minutes to go before the bus was due to leave Adam returned. He had got lost but found his way back.

One thing I remember about the trip was that the food was quite bland. The milk is processed so that it lasts for six months on the shelf – yuk! You did not know if you were buying whipped cream or shaving cream. I could not read or speak French.

After spending a week there with no watch I arranged for a taxi to pick me up at 6 a.m. I had to stay awake as I did not know the correct time. We caught a train to Paris, arrived at the station, put the big suitcases in the security lockers and walked a few blocks from the station. We booked into a hotel and proceeded to set off to see the Eiffel Tower at night. I had seen it when on the 1972 tour in the daytime and thought it was very impressive.

We decided to head back to the hotel. We noticed a lot of homeless people in the park. We took the Metro back towards the centre. At night the stores pull down the metal blinds for security reasons so I lost my bearings as to where our hotel was. There was no name or phone number on the keys. Fortunately it was a warm night. I got a taxi and told Adam to wait in the café. That did not help and it cost me US$100 so I said to Adam that we would wait until daylight and then retrace our steps from the station. We did. We were just about to ask a policewoman for help when Adam looked to his right and noticed the hotel about 50 yards away. We were never so happy to see something. It was like we had won the lottery. We ran in grabbed our stuff and took off to catch the Eurostar to London.

As we were walking down the street on the other side I noticed that the building was the headquarters for the French Rugby Union. The next day was the semifinal between France and New Zealand. France were 16/1 underdogs to win so you stood to win a lot of dollars if you bet on France. My nephew, Jason, got us the tickets for the game and gave Adam and me souvenir rugby shirts plus he put us up. I am forever grateful.

Me, Adam and Jason (he has lost a lot of weight since this photo was taken)

We went across for the first time through the 'Chunnel' under the English Channel which is an amazing engineering feat. It was total darkness. It connects to the London train and underground system. We met Jason at the pub right beside the station.

The next day we watched our beloved All Blacks lose to France after having a big lead at half time. Was that a bad omen based on what happened to us in Paris? There was an English guy in front of us with a Kiwi friend. He was cheering on New Zealand when they were winning when all of a sudden the tide turned and the French were getting the better of the All Blacks. Then he started yelling "come on Northern Hemisphere." What a turncoat!

I put Adam on the plane back to the US and went and watched the All Blacks in Cardiff, Wales at the new Millennium Stadium. It has a retractable roof. I stayed at Jason's Uncle Gerald's house. Gerald took me to the area in Newport, Wales which had a museum with all the relics they had dug up from the early Roman days. The area across from the museum had the shape of a coliseum which had been overgrown by grass over the centuries.

With Paul at his house………. He died two months after these photos were taken.

Me in front of 118 Clermiston Avenue where we grew up. It hasn't changed since we lived here.

At the back of Clermiston Avenue. I am flanked by Josh and Esther Phillip's children. Where we are standing is an empty lot where as children, Peter, Philip, Stephen and I, together with our friends, would dig a huge hole in the ground and cover it to make a hut. Nobody seemed to object. Also to the right was a Baptist Church where the Minister would take all the kids for a trip in his van on Sundays.

Chapter Ten

Confirming the Switch – and Then What?

The huge, life-changing secret came out of the closet in 2002. And the thread that started to unravel this huge secret was a history of heart problems in the George family. Paul and my mother had died of heart attacks. And my brother Stephan had undergone bypass heart surgery. There have been no problems on my George sisters. So it was clear heart trouble runs in the George male side of the family, even though I had never had any heart problem myself, of course! Thank God Neville & Peter have had no problems pertaining to there heart.

Then Jim Churchman had a heart attack followed by heart bypass surgery. As a young boy Jim had suspected he might belong to another family but his Dad made a cursory inquiry with the doctor and told his son to forget about those thoughts. But forgetting is not always easy. It was because of his close friendship with my older brother Michael that Jim had noticed how many similarities he shared with the George family. Because the Churchmans did not have any medical heart issues, and the George family did, Jim began to have second thoughts about his family tree.

By 2002 Michael is dead so Jim Churchman makes contact with my brother Phillip and shares some of his thoughts and suspicions. Phillip decides to get involved. I was coming to New Zealand in 2002 for a visit and Phillip, at Jim's instigation and with his approval, asks me to take a blood test during my visit. So when I arrived in Dunedin, Phillip went with me to the clinic and I had the blood test done. Jim also went to a lab and had a blood test. Because Jim was so concerned about his own family's medical history and genetic structure, he paid to have the DNA analyzed in London.

In about a month the DNA results were sent back. The DNA results confirmed without a doubt that I was actually the son of Gordon and Helen Churchman son, and that Jim Churchman was actually the son of John and Ngaire George. The cat was out of the bag and could never crawl back in again. The huge mystery in my life was no longer a secret. I was, indeed, a Swan.

I had returned home to Massachusetts when the results arrived in New Zealand and I was emailed the results on the Internet. The news took my breath away.

Even though the possibility had been discussed at various times, including when Jim and I were 16- or 17-years-old, I still was not prepared for the findings.

Because I was back home in Massachusetts when the DNA results came through Jim Churchman learned about the switch at birth just a little before I did. My daughter Jessica, however, was visiting in New Zealand at that time. Jim, who was concerned about how best to tell "our" mother the truth about our births and the switch, approached Jessica with an idea. Jim thought that it would soften the blow if he introduced Jessie to Helen Churchman as her granddaughter. So he made arrangements for the surprise.

Jim went to visit Helen Churchman and took Jessie along with him. When they first went in and saw Mrs. Churchman, Jim didn't introduce Jessie. Instead he said to his mother, "Sit down, Mum, and let me get you something to drink."

Although Helen Churchman was 82-years-old at the time, this is no moss-covered granny we're dealing with here. She was quite sharp and to this day remains quite sharp. She thinks to herself, "What's going on? It's pretty early in the morning for drinks."

Then Jim said, "I have a surprise for you. You have a beautiful granddaughter." And he brought Jessica forward and introduced her.

Helen Churchman's thought was, "What has Jim been up to now? Has he had an affair? Is this his illegitimate daughter?"

Then Jim started to unravel this huge, life-changing secret to the mother who raised him. It was a huge shock for her but she graciously and heartily welcomed Jessie heartily once she understood what was happening.

And that is how my daughter got to meet my mother before I did.

Once we had the DNA results – concrete, undeniable proof that a terrible mistake had been made 57 years before – other things started to come together.

In hindsight we could see that Jim really has the George temperament. He is willing to take risks, including in business, and he conducts business like the Lebanese. My Churchman cousins have told me, "How amazing that Jim does these daring things." And I find myself thinking, "That's no surprise – he's really a George." Temperamentally, I've always been more conservative and have always been more like a Churchman.

If you take photographs of Jim and photographs of me and place alongside the Churchman and George family photographs the results are obvious and undeniable. Jim looks just like the Georges, and I look just like the Churchmans.

There was another chance encounter with Jim Churchman when I was a young man. I was at my sister Nora's apartment and met a girl who invited me to a party the next evening. She suggested I pick her up at her parent's house. So after meeting her parents, obviously to get there approval, the young lady and I arrived at the party.

I didn't know anyone at the party except for Jim Churchman and his wife, Marge. The young lady was ignoring me when this long-haired, scruffy guy confronted me with some pretty menacing looks. While I was wondering what was going on, Jim steps in, and using the guy's name asks him to leave me alone as I hadn't meant any harm. Little did I know that the young lady was using me to make her boyfriend jealous and jealous he did get! Looking back I wonder if Jim at the time viewed me as his brother's brother, which I would not find until years later I was or as a young brother who needed his protection.

When I was 10- or 12-years-old I had a notion that I wanted to be a missionary. I had no where that idea came from. Now I know that there are lots of ministers in the Churchman-Somerville family. Helen Churchman's brother, brother-in-law and nephew were all ministers. In fact, one of those "coincidences" happened when I was in elementary school, regarding Helen Churchman's brother – the Rev. Tom Somerville, pastor of the Presbyterian Church in Green Island. That church is near where Saint Peter Chanel School is. Not long ago I returned to Dunedin and talked with a couple of the nuns from my times who were still at St. Peter

Chanel School. The nuns had known Pastor Tom Somerville as a good minister and pretty popular man.

Owen Churchman, the brother who was born after Jim, had a blood test done that confirmed that is a Churchman. So Owen is my full brother. Owen not only looks like me but has the same voice. I listen to his voice, and listen to my own, and it's clear that we talk exactly the same way. My son Adam also sounds the same way. Owen and I also share the same peculiar mannerism when we meet people. We're really quite shy and we kind of hide behind our fingers at first. It looks like we're maybe picking our nose or scratching our face but we're really trying to hide.

Owen and I both have these lumps on our bodies, called lymphomas (fatty tissue), which I discovered when I was in my 20s. My doctor cut one of them out and had an analysis done; fortunately it was benign and no cause for concern. I even went into the hospital and had it checked out. Before I found out I was paranoid, as I thought it may be cancerous. I never told anybody about my fear.

Even though Mrs. Churchman lost me because of the switch, she received a carbon copy of me two years later- in Owen.

I write just like my birth mother – the same as the ancient Egyptians. Sometimes I can't read my own writing.

Jim Churchman *acts* like he's a George and always has. But, than, he always has been a George.

My brother Paul, who was always a scrapper, used to wear old clothes when he went out because he figured he'd be in a fight before he left the party. A year or so ago, Paul and his wife had gone out with Jim and I for the evening. Sure enough, an altercation broke out. And Jim was right in the middle of it with Paul – giving as good as he got. He's really a George!

Well, it was exciting right at first to learn I never really *was* a George after all but was a Churchman all that time. But, after the initial excitement cooled, I was left dealing with the question of where to go from here?

In spite of the switch at birth, Ngaire George was my saviour. She nursed me through all those illnesses when I was an infant and a toddler. She had an extremely hard life with such a large huge family and so little money or support. She had a nervous breakdown, and was in and out of institutions. But she was always loyal to me. When any question about my looks came up, Mum simply said she was just convinced that I was a throwback to her Scandinavian ancestors. It's funny but Helen Churchman had a similar rationalization about Jim's dark looks; she thought he was a throwback to her own darker-featured Welsh ancestors.

While Mum knew she was of Scandinavian descent, she like me did not know the entire story of her birth family. Mum was fostered out as a baby and raised by step-parents so she knew little about her birth parents.

She thought she was Norwegian but was actually Swedish. Years after Mum died, my brother Phillip did some genealogy research and learned that Ngaire George's last name was really Pearson. Her mother was a Pearson and her grandfather, also a Pearson, came from Sweden. Mum didn't know anything about these relatives; she also had a brother she didn't know. While I am intrigued that Mum also had relatives she did not know and a family history kept secret from her, I also am intrigued that the midwife who laid Jim and me in the wrong crib in the hospital also was a descendent of the Pearsons from Sweden. I have no idea if the midwife's Pearsons were any relation at all to the Pearsons on Ngaire George's family tree. At this point I just don't know!

Ngaire George died in 1970, John George died in 1980, and Gordon Churchman died in 1982. So none of them ever knew for sure about the switch at birth.

The only one of the parents still alive is Helen Churchman, now 85-years-old. Imagine the blow it must have been to learn at age 82 that the man you knew for 56 years as your son was not your son. She's really the one who has taken the hardest knock; it's a bigger shock for her than anyone else.

My birth mother and I write back and forth to each other now, every week. And we talk on the phone once in a while. But it's extremely hard to form a relationship with somebody you don't know, even if she is your mother.

When we first found out definitely about the switch, of course, it was a shock for everyone and no one knew quite what to. But most everyone has been supportive, and has tried to help and understand.

My birth mother, Helen Churchman, wrote this "testimonial" that was distributed at her 85th birthday party:

When I was 80, my sister gave me a huge helium filled balloon with "Today I am 80" plastered all over it. I was so embarrassed all I could think was "How can I get this monstrosity home without being noticed?" I slithered it behind my back, down the steps of the restaurant. It kept going sideways and when I reached the bottom it blew away! Later, it was returned to me with the remark "It must be awfully old to be 80!" All I wanted to do then was to get this thing into a dark cupboard and let it shrink way to nothing. But now I am 85 my attitude has changed dramatically. I am glad to be alive and it's a good life at 85. If you see me with 85 on my shoes, 85 on my handbag and even 85 on my letterbox, you will know I am celebrating!

Tonight, I really want Fred to be centre stage – coming all the way from Boston, leaving Paula, Jessica and Adam behind to visit his family and come to the birthday celebration. Thank you, Fred. You will all know about Fred and Jim. It was Jim who rang in November last year to say, "Mum, I'm in Dunedin on business and will see you in a few minutes". I could only think, "How strange - Jim never comes on business!" But maybe, since Dunedin is fast becoming the Riviera of the South, there could be a need for spa pools! He +arrived in his usual cheerful way, suggested I sit down and poured me a sherry – strange in the morning? There was much more to come with the punch line – "How would you like to have another granddaughter?" I knew Jim was a hard-case but I didn't expect him to go as far as that! Then with more unravelling, it turns out that I do have a new granddaughter 'Jessica', I do have a new grandson 'Adam' and I do have a new daughter-in-law 'Paula' and a long lost son, 'Fred'.

Fred isn't entirely new to me. I got to know him in the Dunedin maternity ward 59 years ago and then he disappeared! Jim appeared out of the blue and I have known Jim for all of his 59 years. At this stage, I would like to thank Fred for helping to lessen the huge gap we all feel, especially Oscar, in the loss of Max. Remember Fred, whenever you visit Clifford St, please don't knock; open the door and walk in and make Clifford St your home.

Helen

This is were my birth mother lives today and were I would have been brought up had I not been switched at birth......Amen!

The Churchmans are more reserved and withdrawn than the Georges. My nephews and nieces on the George side have been supportive, as have my brothers and sisters on the George side. But the new and old relationships are quite hard to deal with. On the one hand you can't act like nothing has happened. On the other hand, you can't throw away a lifetime of relationships, either. I would not change my past for anything.

In a way, I wonder if all this really matters so much. After all, I've lived in the United States, separated from both families, longer than I lived in New Zealand. But I was brought up in the middle of the Georges. Mother, father, aunts, uncles, brothers, sisters, nieces, nephews – you can't just tear that away. And it's the same for Jim, now. How could he possibly break away from the family he grew up with?

At work, you have relationships with the people on your job. You may even get to be good friends with some. But if you leave the job or get fired, or they leave or get fired, ties are cut right there but it's not the end of the world. But you can't do that with the family you were brought up with.

I can't break away from my history. I love these people. I've grown up with these people. I can't leave them, or trade them in as you might do with an old shoe -- "off with the old, on with the new." I would have been the second oldest of the Churchman children, but I'm right in the middle of the George family. I have very close relationships with my younger and older brothers and sisters on the George side.

My son Adam is fascinated by this turn of events. He has gone to New Zealand and met the Churchman cousins and the George "cousins." He has been able to forge relationships with them all.

There are things both Jim and I have missed out on that can never be replaced or made up for. Jim, for instance, has been denied his Lebanese heritage and the spiritual influence of the Roman Catholic Church. He had some experience of the closeness of the George family, though. He and Michael were good friends for most of their lives, and Jim knew all the rest of us pretty well.

This photo was taken at the Lebanese Cedar Club. Too many people to name. They are my George siblings, aunts, cousins, nephews and nieces. I am 5th from the back (blue sweater) from right.

This is a picture of the George's and Churchman's in-laws and friends taken in the back of Mrs. Churchman's house in North Dunedin

Above: (front row): Me, Jim Churchman, Paula

The George family group – the children of John and Ngaire.

My birth mother – Helen Churchman – and me taken at St Clair Beach, Dunedin.

My daughter, Jessica with her 'grandmother' – Helen Churchman.

Jessica was in New Zealand when the DNA results came through to officially confirm that Helen Churchman (Jim's mum) was in fact my birth mother. She would meet my birth mother before me.

Jenny, Jody, Jan and Owen Churchman

Left to right: Me, with my Churchman brothers, Jock, Jim and Owen

James Francis Churchman (known as Jim) born 24/12/46 with his family, Gabriel, Marcelle and his wife, Margie. He was actually born on the 23rd Dec. at 11.55 p.m. Fred was born on the 24th at 1.38 a.m.

Matt George (Neville's son), Paula, Gabriel (Jim's son), Jim Churchman and me in front.

The twins – Phillip and Peter George

This is where my mother and father are buried. Notice the grave to the left is Patie Byrne (Irishman) who was married to our cousin, Madeline.

I don't have any relationship at all with Owen. I have talked to Jane on the phone and she sends me a Christmas card every year. Before this huge secret was unveiled by DNA, Jane had met the George brothers and had a strong suspicion that Jim was there brother. But Jane was not in a position to do anything about it.

I never met Max Churchman, one of Owen's brothers, because he died of non-Hodgkin's lymphoma in 1989. I have since met Max's wife, Hilary, and their

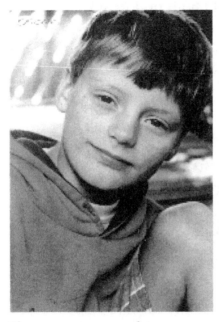

son Oscar (pictured here). Hilary has been through some tough times. When Max was sick with non-Hodgkin's lymphoma, their daughter, Serena, was also sick with a form of leukaemia. Thankfully Serena recovered. Max was the youngest in the Churchman family. When I went to Wellington it was a pleasure to meet Hilary. She was very good to me.

A couple of my George brothers met Max years ago. Because he worked for the New Zealand Wool Company, Max had learned to speak Chinese fluently and he quite popular with the Chinese. In fact, some of the Chinese people he got to know were so fond of him that they named their children after him. So if you're ever in China and you meet a Chinese boy with the name of Max – well, now you'll know where he got his name.

Jock Churchman is the oldest Churchman son. He is a soil scientist, and just a couple of years ago was in Philadelphia at a scientific conference. He came to Pembroke and stayed at our place for a few days. It takes time and effort to work out new family relationships. Jock has been great since he found out we were brothers. But Jock and I both find it awkward to talk about "our" relations. Jock and his wife Jan actually lived in the United States before I came to this country. In fact while driving to Cape Cod once they drove by Pembroke, the town I live in now.

Gordon John Churchman (known as Jock) born 23/5/44 with his family and wife, Janice Winter.

Jim is a friend but we never became close. He was always closer to my brother Michael. Jim is extremely business-minded -- very Lebanese in that regard. We don't often talk on the phone, but we do email each other frequently.

A fascinating thread that runs deep through my entire switched at birth saga is the impact that genetics has had. I have come to appreciate that our genes control much more of us than we understand or appreciate.

The huge secret of who I really was at birth was uncovered by DNA which is like a set of fingerprints of our genetic makeup. Studies on the importance of genetics reveal that we not only inherit much more from our parents than previously imagined. We do inherit our parent's body traits such as hair and eye color, shape of ears, baldness, buckteeth, height, weight and body shape. We also inherit their medical frailties – tendencies to have heart disease, diabetes, cancer, etc. But we also inherit our parents' traits, mannerisms, idiosyncrasies, inclinations, and personalities.

Genes are like a weed that spread through the family garden patch from one sibling to another. That became quite clear to me after seeing my birth brother for the first time in 57 years. We are so much alike in so many ways that other people, many of them strangers to me, can see how alike Owen and I are.

When I share my switched at birth story with other people I often receive feedback that adds further credence to the powerful force our genetic makeup is in determining who we *really* are. For example, a woman has a three-year-old grand-daughter with a mole under her left foot and the woman's son (the grand-daughter's uncle) also has a mole under his left foot. And so the genes we inherit are like a weed that spreads from siblings to siblings in our immediate garden patch but also spreads over the fields to future generations.

One thing that does bother me, though, is religion. Every time I get out my books on the Somerville family, and my books on the George family, I can't avoid seeing that they each subscribe to a totally different religious faith.

Growing up in the George family, I was a devout Catholic. That stayed with me through my whole life. I always went to mass on Sunday, made regular confessions and said the rosary -- although I didn't do it every night on my knees, the way Aunty Jean used to have us do.

But now I know that if the switch hadn't happened I would have been raised to be a devout Presbyterian. And so now I wonder about religion. What is it and how does it impact me personally? I've lost the will and devoutness I had before. I have lost the will to go to church. I just don't know where I really belong.

I still have faith in God and still want to be a good person. I still believe in trying to do good things for other people. Paula volunteers for *Toys for Tots*, and I contribute to Jimmy Carter's charity in Africa. I donate blood to the Red Cross regularly. I'm trying to help my brothers and sisters in New Zealand by sending money the ones that need it. I also volunteered on weekends in the middle of winter to help build a house for *Habitat For Humanity* in a town in Massachusetts. It was so cold on one particular day that when one of the guys spilt his coffee on the ground it turned into ice in a matter of seconds. But I did not notice the cold as we were doing some good for humanity. I used to make a big pot of stew and bring it in to my fellow workers.

I still have thoughts of becoming a missionary. A lot of my ancestors have been ministers, and I keep thinking about that. But religion and how it impacts us individually is not predictable. You go along in your regular life, and then something really dramatic happens and you have no control over whether it happens, how long it lasts, or when it stops. I once had an experience in the middle of the night where I saw a vision of Jesus Christ, and heard Him call my name. Another time, I was working at landscaping for some people we knew. I was mowing the lawn when I had a vision of the Blessed Virgin Mary. She appeared on the window of the house. So you never know how, when or why God deals with you.

Right now, I am just trying live a day at a time. None of this changes *me*, really. None of it changes who I am in my heart and soul. My wife, my children are just the same -- the switch at birth doesn't really have any effect on their lives.

I'm really proud of my kids. Adam has worked hard for all he has. And he knows his own mind. He's a good man. Jessie is a hard worker, and takes her jobs seriously. She has just become a mother and we are really enjoying being grandparents! I love my family. And this I know with absolute certainty -- that I love them whether I'm a George or a Churchman.

One lighter footnote to this story. Whenever the police pull me over for speeding or whatever, I just say to them:*"You have the wrong guy."* They can't argue with that!

So is it possible, after all – after all this time, after all this thought, after everything – is it possible that the switch didn't really <u>matter</u>? I wonder.

While clearly I don't know all the answers there are some messages I can share with complete clarity. And one such truth is the compelling message that the power of genetics is an important force that controls much more than physical traits. Genetics defines who we are much more than we think. This is important to everyone, but especially to anyone who has been adopted, fostered out to another family, or switched at birth.

For those who struggle with identity issues it is important that they be themselves and not try to conform to the ways of their new parents or new siblings or new friends. The truth is that their new parents, siblings and friends love them for whom they really are and so there is no need to change. Just be who you are because it is your genes that have a lot to do in determining who you are. So your birth parents will have an impact on who you are and how you act, even if you have never met them. Someone adopted out or fostered out as a newborn who years later meet their birth parents will, by genetic makeup, already have a lot in common. There will be no need to change to be more like your newly-discovered birth parents because you already like them. So it's rather silly to try to conform to someone whom is different than yourself.

We all have heard of children, teens or adults for whom meeting their birth parents for the first time is a traumatic event. But they never step away from the initial trauma, and continue to wallow in the abyss of emotions that initially swept over them, that they are unable to get on with life. They spend years in psychological counselling and therapy – struggling to become someone whom they already are!

I am not opposed to counselling and certainly recommend seeking professional help when, if, and as needed. But we can save lot of money, trouble, effort and time if we simply accept who we are from the earliest point possible after learning the identity of our birth parents and birth family. Somehow we have to move on; we cannot wallow in the moment and become emotionally stagnant. You were a good person before you learned the truth of your biological identity; you are still a good person now and will be in the years ahead. Simply accept that you are who you are and move on with the wonderful life you have and the many wonderful opportunities that lay ahead.

Learn to be content with who you are and with your station in life. In one of his letters, St. Paul writes: *"I have learned whatsoever state I am in therein to be content."* That's some pretty powerful advice that would be good for all of us to follow.

I can do nothing now about the fact that a hospital nurse 57 years ago placed me in the wrong bassinet. I can only accept that the next morning I was carried from the hospital crib to the wrong mother's arms. DNA proves that's what happened; why should I struggle with the absolute certainty that I was switched at birth. Is there anything else I can or should do but accept what happened and get over the crisis? I do have a new mother to get acquainted with and I have new brothers to build relationships with. But I have old relationships, also, with my George siblings to cherish and embrace. And so I choose to be content with the life I have and will continue to love, honor and cherish my wonderful wife, children, and grandchild.

This is the lesson I have learned and this is the message I wish to share with anyone who struggles with their identity. We are whom we are so be whom we are! Be yourself and do not to conform to your new siblings or to anyone else for that matter.

Epilogue:

Maurice Hugh Frederick Wilkins was born in New Zealand, grew up in England, and as a young man studied at Birmingham University. As a physicist Wilkins helped develop the nuclear bomb. After seeing what the nuclear bomb did to Japan and the Japanese people, Wilkins transferred to the genetics department of Birmingham University in 1946, the year Jim Churchman and I were born. *(Coincidently my father-in law's commanding officer, Major Charles Sweeney, flew one of the planes that dropped the nuclear bombs on Nagasaki, Japan).*

At Birmingham University Maurice Wilkins, working with colleague Roseland Franklin, started a genetics research project in the mid-1940s that culminated years later in the application of DNA to positively confirm identifies. Their research pinpointed a large molecule with the substance DNA wrapped around it with a glass stirring rod molecule, and observed under a microscope. Wilkins was the first to extract a thin strand from the DNA, a strand

containing the genetic roadmap of that human being.
After developing the double helix, James Watson
and Francis Crick conferred with Wilkins and Franklin
and solidified their discovery of the double helix.
Wilkins, Watson and Crick received the Noble Prize
Laureate for Physiology and Medicine for their
discoveries. Franklin had died before the awards.
Franklin had died of cancer, probably caused by her
being exposed to radiation with X-rays diffractions.

Since then other scientists have copied the initial
findings of Wilkins. There is something like 30,000 genes
in the human genome. DNA, as a whole, is long
enough to go from here to the moon many times.

Using a Wilkins/ Franklin X-ray diffraction picture
of the DNA molecule, Crick and Watson were able to
build their correct and detailed model of the double
helix which were released in the medical journals in
1953 also the same year Sir Edmund Hillary of New
Zealand and his guide became the first humans to climb
the highest mountain in the world, Mount Everest. And
1953 was the same year as the coronation of the Queen
of England.

Sir Edmund Hillary did a lot of benevolent good
for the Nepal people, building hospital clinics and
schools for the locals of the Himalayas which was his
way of paying them back, with financial help from the
New Zealand and U.S.A. governments. Sir Edmund just
died in January 2008.

Made in the USA
Middletown, DE
24 July 2021